Frozen Foods Cookbook

Now you can simplify your meal preparations and menu planning — and enhance the pleasures of home cooking with this convenient FROZEN FOODS COOKBOOK from General Foods Kitchens. All of the recipes (more than 200!) feature time-saving frozen vegetables, fruits, and/or juice concentrates; all have that exciting "something special" to tempt your family and guests.

For the adventurous cook, we've included a seasoning and flavoring guide, and we've suggested new horizons for your own creative ability with the saucepan. Because no one ever has enough pre-meal fussing time, most of the recipes include do-it-beforehand tips; these suggestions show clearly which part of the recipe can be prepared early — to eliminate last-minute rush.

We've tried, too, to anticipate your questions on frozen foods. In addition to the recipes, the FROZEN FOODS COOKBOOK includes charts and information telling:

What temperatures are best for storing frozen foods

How long you can keep frozen foods

How various foods rate nutritionally

You'll find this handy book attractive and appealing — as well as informative — since it's lavishly illustrated with both black-and-white and full-color photographs.

Our General Foods Kitchens staff includes parents, homemakers and consumers just like you and your neighbors. We also have technicians, home economists, nutrition experts, and scientists who hail from all sections of the country, reflecting tastes very similar to yours. So here's a cookbook that should be a useful companion in everyone's kitchen.

Best Frozen Foods Sources of Nutrients

Vitamin A
Peas and Carrots
Spinach
Collard Greens
Kale
Turnip Greens
Mixed Vegetables
Winter Squash
Sweet Potatoes
Broccoli
Apricots

Thiamine
Pork
Black-Eye Peas
Green Peas
Peas and Carrots
Asparagus
Corn
Okra
Citrus Juices

Riboflavin
Meats
Poultry
Salmon
Oysters
Okra
Spinach
Collard Greens

Kale
Turnip Greens
Asparagus
Broccoli
Black-Eye Peas
Brussels Sprouts
Green Beans

Niacin
Poultry
Fish
Potatoes
Green Peas
Corn
Peas and Carrots
Succotash
Mixed Vegetables
Black-Eye Peas
Asparagus
Lima Beans
Green Beans

**Ascorbic Acid
(Vitamin C)**
Citrus Juices
Grapefruit Sections
Brussels Sprouts
Broccoli
Strawberries
Spinach

Collard Greens
Kale
Turnip Greens
Cauliflower

Protein
Poultry
Meats
Sea Foods
Meat Pies
Plate Dinners
Black-Eye Peas
Lima Beans
Green Peas
Corn
Broccoli
Brussels Sprouts
Asparagus
Peas and Carrots
Succotash
Mixed Vegetables

Calcium
Collard Greens
Kale
Turnip Greens
Okra
Broccoli
Green Beans
Lima Beans

Iron
Meats
Black-Eye Peas
Lima Beans
Spinach
Collard Greens
Kale
Turnip Greens
Mixed Vegetables
Green Peas
Potatoes

**Frozen Fruits
and Vegetables
Low in Sodium**
Asparagus
Green Beans
Wax Beans
Corn*
Grapefruit Juice
Okra*
Orange Juice
Peaches
Black-Eye Peas
Potatoes*
Red Raspberries
Strawberries
Winter Squash
Yellow Crookneck
 Squash*

*When processed without salt

General Foods Kitchens

FROZEN FOODS COOKBOOK

(Modern Living with Frozen Foods)

BY GENERAL FOODS KITCHENS

Drawings by MARY RONIN *and* WILLIAM RONIN
Cover photographs by NORMAN KARLSON

RANDOM HOUSE

Front Cover Illustrations: Spinach-Stuffed Tomatoes (p. 32), Pickabacks (p. 6), Orange-Glazed Pork Chops (p. 17) served with Butter-Boil Lima Beans (p. 41), Crisscross Pie (p. 61).

Back Cover Illustrations: Strawberry Punch (p. 74) with frozen peaches floated on top, Spring Corn (p. 37), Salad Vinaigrette (p. 50), and Strawberry Shortcake (p. 58).

Contents

Foreword	THE FROZEN FOODS STORY	v
Introduction	MODERN LIVING WITH FROZEN FOODS	vii
Section I.	APPETIZERS	1
Section II.	ENTRÉES	9
Section III.	VEGETABLES	29
Section IV.	SALADS	45
Section V.	DESSERTS	55
Section VI.	FRUIT DRINKS	69
Section VII.	DELICIOUS THIS-AND-THAT	77
Section VIII.	JELLIES AND JAMS	85
Section IX.	COOKOUT CAPERS	91
Section X.	SEASONING AND FLAVORING GUIDE	96
	INDEX	102

The Frozen Foods Story

The story of any industry is the story of many people — their imagination, resourcefulness, struggles, successes. But often one man stands out because through a chance incident he conceived an idea *and pursued it*.

Many years ago, Clarence Birdseye, an American explorer in Labrador, found that fish caught through the ice in below-zero temperatures froze almost before he could take them off the hook. When thawed and cooked months later, the fish had the firmness and delicacy of a new catch. He judged — and rightly — that it was the very  rapid freezing in extreme cold that preserved the fresh qualities. He saw possibilities for freezing fish in his native New England and shipping them all over the United States.

Earlier researchers had developed a way to quick-freeze foods but considered it impractical for commercial use. Clarence Birdseye set out to improve their methods. And so began a new industry.

At first he worked alone but later joined with two other researchers. And by 1926 they were ready to ship to market. Unfortunately, the American housewife was not ready to buy. She did not then understand the difference between cold storage foods — of which she was wary — and this new safe food. Stores had no way to keep foods frozen and still display them. Truckers and railroad operators had no means of shipping at the necessary low temperatures.

The infant industry needed more capital. And so in 1929, Clarence Birdseye and his associates turned over their patents and operations to what is now General Foods.

The new campaign to win consumer confidence began with orders solicited by phone . . . food demonstrations in stores . . . and door-to-door canvassing to explain quick-frozen foods to housewives. In some communities, a truck circulated the neighborhoods, selling the foods directly.

So, step by step, the operation expanded . . . acquired processing plants, farms, trawler fleets, laboratories for research, warehouses . . . solved shipping problems . . . designed frozen-food cabinets for stores.

Success came slowly at first, and there were many set-backs. But during World War II, women by the thousands, busy in war work, discovered the quality and convenience of frozen foods. Men and women in the armed forces, too, discovered their quality.

Today, frozen foods have helped to improve the eating habits of a nation and to provide a year-round abundance unheard of sixty years ago.

Birds Eye is still the largest processor and distributor of frozen foods. And the quest for ever better methods goes on. The years ahead will see many new and exciting frozen foods on the market. It may be, too, that some current products will be withdrawn, for there are fashions in foods as in everything else. And when taste for a certain food wanes, Birds Eye anticipates the change in vogue and responds at once to provide the homemaker and her family with the best in those foods she most desires.

General Foods Kitchens Frozen Foods Cookbook

MODERN LIVING WITH FROZEN FOODS

A fine meal is more than just good things to eat. For the cook, it's a triumph of skill — made easier today with frozen foods. The fruit cup's frosty cold. The chicken's golden brown and tender. Peas and squash are delectably seasoned and piping hot. *And everything's ready at once.*

The modern secret of successful meal preparation lies not only in learning how to plan and cook well but how to save time with modern foods. In compiling this book, we at General Foods Kitchens selected recipes that take advantage of frozen-foods convenience. For with frozen foods the dull part of cookery — the hulling, paring, washing, and cutting — is already accomplished. The enjoyable part remains permitting all sorts of creative cookery.

The frozen food recipes here run the gamut from soups to stews to stuffings to soufflés to sauces to . . . well . . . just about everything, plain and fancy. Most of them may be made in advance. If not whole recipes, at least parts can be fixed in the early morning or the night before. We've tagged these with a *prepare-ahead hint,* intended especially for beginners.

Look, too, for the ways to experiment with herbs and spices, and the various charts planned for your day-by-day use.

ABOUT NUTRITION

Reliable brands of frozen foods are bound to be nutritious. Why? Because responsible processors do everything possible to select only top-quality foods and protect them through the whole process of quick-freezing.

Take fruits and vegetables, for instance. Scientists discover the best varieties for color, flavor, tenderness, nutritive value, and ability to stay fresh. And these are specially grown for freezing. So that only the finest raw foods — of whatever kind — are frozen.

Crops of fruits and vegetables are harvested at the exact moment of ripeness; then processed at once. *For the food that is frozen, time stops. And the nutritive goodness and garden freshness are literally frozen in.*

On the way to the grocer's frozen food department, the packaged foods stay solidly frozen in refrigerated cars and trucks.

Each package of Birds Eye foods carries directions thoroughly tested by General Foods Kitchens (and often recipes or serving suggestions, too) to help you prepare the food properly.

On the inside cover, you will find a chart, showing the best frozen food sources of vitamins and minerals.

AVERAGE SERVINGS OF FROZEN FOODS AS SOURCES OF RECOMMENDED DAILY DIETARY ALLOWANCES

(Based on research by the Wisconsin Alumni Research Foundation at Madison, Wisconsin)

FROZEN FOODS	VITAMINS					MINERALS	
	C	A*	Niacin	Riboflavin	Thiamine	Iron	Sodium
Broccoli	Exc.	Good	Appreciable	Appreciable	Appreciable	Appreciable	Moderately Low
Beans, Green	—	Good	Appreciable	Appreciable	Appreciable	Appreciable	Low
Beans, Lima	Good	—	Good	Appreciable	Appreciable	Good	—
Corn	—	—	Good	Appreciable	Appreciable	Appreciable	Low
Grapefruit Juice	Exc.	—	Appreciable	—	Appreciable	—	Low
Orange Juice	Exc.	—	Appreciable	—	Good	—	Low
Peaches	Good	—	Appreciable	—	—	—	Low
Peas	Good	Good	Good	Appreciable	Good	Good	—
Red Raspberries	Good	—	Appreciable	Appreciable	—	Appreciable	Low
Spinach	Good	Exc.	Appreciable	Good	Appreciable	Good	—
Strawberries	Exc.	—	Appreciable	Appreciable	—	Appreciable	Low

*Measured as beta-carotene.

Excellent (Exc.):	From 70% to 185% of Recommended Daily Dietary Allowances
Good:	From 11% to 30% of Recommended Daily Dietary Allowances
Appreciable:	From 5% to 10% of Recommended Daily Dietary Allowances
Iron—Good:	From 10% to 25% of Recommended Daily Dietary Allowances
Appreciable:	From 5% to 10% of Recommended Daily Dietary Allowances
Sodium:	Low contains from 0.3 to 8.3 mg.; Moderately Low contains from 11 to 26 mg.

FROZEN FOOD Q&A

Now and then at General Foods Kitchens we receive such questions as these:

How long will frozen foods keep?

To answer, we have compiled a chart of recommended storage times (see inside cover). Note that the best temperature for storage is 0°F. or less. But foods will keep safely for a month or so at 20°F. though they lose freshness in color, flavor, and texture much faster than when stored at the ideal temperature.

Is it ever safe to refreeze foods?

Yes, if fruits and vegetables are only slightly thawed and the package still feels thoroughly cold to the hand. But plan to use them ahead of your other frozen foods.

Thoroughly thawed fruits and vegetables, when refrozen, tend to lose quality quickly. So treat the recently thawed foods as you do fresh ones — that is, prepare and serve them before their freshness is gone. Never refreeze ground meat, chicken livers, fish, shell fish, or other such perishables. If they've been stored at 0°F. and recently thawed, use them up soon, again, just as you would fresh foods.

When you're not sure how long a food has been thawed . . . well . . . that's another story. Foods may spoil when they thaw slowly over several days and warm to a temperature of 40°F. or more. Be especially wary of meats, poultry, most vegetables, and some prepared foods. Fruits and fruit juices, under these conditions, usually develop a sharp flavor and poor color.

What do you do with frozen foods while defrosting the refrigerator?

Empty ice cubes from trays onto layers of newspaper — (it's excellent insulation); then wrap cubes and frozen food packages together in the paper. Frozen foods may also be stored temporarily in heavy cardboard cartons or insulated bags. Smartest plan, of course, is to defrost when the larder's low, just before shopping and stocking up.

What do you do with a freezer when the power fails?

Your impulse is to look inside and see how the foods are holding up. But don't. Open the freezer only when necessary. If it's fully stocked, foods will stay frozen at least 2 days . . . if only partly stocked, about 1 day. Suppose the power interruption lasts more than a day or two? Buy dry ice, allowing 25 pounds for a 10-cubic-foot cabinet. Leave ice in as large chunks as possible and place on top of the foods. They should then stay safely frozen for 2 to 4 days.

Is a freezer a good investment?

For convenience, most certainly. When you own a freezer you can: Save shopping time by shopping less often. Buy foods in quantity at less cost. Take advantage of special sales on top-quality foods. Cook and bake at your leisure. Be ready for unexpected guests or emergencies. Entertain more easily. Help on community suppers, food bazaars, school teas, and so on with less fuss.

For thrifty use, keep your freezer well stocked and rotate the foods. For instance, when you buy commercially frozen foods and plan to store them, date the packages when you get them home from the grocery, and place them in the freezer *under* packages of earlier date. That way, when you take off the top package, you're always sure of using up foods in the order of purchase.

For two-in-the-family, what's the best way to use frozen vegetables?

Some frozen vegetables — peas and green beans, for instance — are loose-packed so that the amount needed for one meal can be easily shaken out of the package and the rest stored.

To break frozen blocks of vegetables, strike the package against a hard surface such as the edge of the kitchen sink or table. (Spinach you may have to cut with a sharp knife.) Cook whatever is needed for one meal and wrap the rest tightly in foil or transparent saran. Store again in freezer.

Sometimes you may prefer to cook the full package, serve part, and fix the rest in a different way for another meal — with a hint of onion, spice, or herb or in a cream sauce or salad.

YOUR OWN TOUCH

Whenever you serve frozen dinners, you can still give the meal your own creative touch. Here are suggestions:

Garnish heat-and-serve meals with *parsley, water cress, radish roses, tender green onions, crisp French fried onion rings, carrot curls, slender celery strips, tomato wedges, thin rings of green pepper, olives — stuffed, green* or *ripe —* or *spiced crab apples, pear,* or *peach.*

Sprinkle vegetable with *chopped chive* or *parsley.* Sprinkle meat with a grind of *fresh pepper* and potato with *paprika.*

Arrange the heated foods on your own pretty dinner plates.

Serve with a hot soup, fruit cup, or fruit shrub; a crisp, mixed green salad, a savory aspic, or fruit salad; hot rolls; jam, jelly or spiced preserves or relish; and a favorite dessert and beverage.

Heat-and-serve meals, like other meals, should have all the elements of a well-planned menu — that is, color, compatible flavors, a contrast of textures, and a variety of foods.

Served hot or cold, easy Vegetable Blender Soups (p. 2) take almost no time to prepare, yet satisfy even gourmets. The version of soup pictured here is made with frozen potato patties.

SECTION 1

GENERAL FOODS KITCHENS

Appetizers

An appetizer is the preamble to the meal and a signal to forget the work-aday world, to relax, and to anticipate the pleasant hours ahead. So appetizers are especially well flavored, often colorful, and always nicely served.

In this section, we offer nibble foods, patés, antipastos, and soups, many of them astonishingly easy to make. This is the course that sets the stage. Be sure the hot things are piping hot, the cold things icy except for dips and such that are meant to be served at room temperature.

GARNISHES

For fruit shrubs: Mint leaf, whole berry, fresh cherries-on-the-stem, orange section, twisted orange slice.

For fruit juices: Floating berries, banana slices, orange, lemon, or lime slices.

For soups: Grated Parmesan cheese, crisp croutons, sieved hard-cooked egg, chopped chive or parsley, or chopped cooked mushroom.

1

For cream soups: Use as garnish large celery leaves, chopped chive or parsley, unsweetened whipped cream or sour cream.

Hearty Beef-Vegetable Chowder

Follow this first course with an omelet, broiled tomato, hot rolls, beverage, and fruit cobbler.

1 pound ground beef
1 cup chopped onions
2 tablespoons butter
2 cups (15½ ounces) canned tomatoes
4 cups hot water
2 bouillon cubes
1 tablespoon salt
⅛ teaspoon pepper
½ bay leaf
1 cup sliced celery
½ teaspoon Worcestershire sauce
1 cup uncooked noodles
1 package (10 ounces) Birds Eye Mixed Garden Vegetables
¼ to ½ teaspoon thyme (optional)

Sauté meat and onions in butter until well browned. Add tomatoes, water, bouillon cubes, salt, pepper, bay leaf, celery, and Worcestershire sauce. Bring to a boil, cover, and simmer 30 minutes. Add noodles, mixed garden vegetables, and thyme. Bring to a boil again and cook 15 minutes. Makes 8 servings. **PREPARE-AHEAD HINT.** Make entire recipe and heat at serving time.

Vegetable Blender Soups

Easiest homemade soups are prepared in electric blender. Good hot or cold.

1 package (10 ounces) Birds Eye Asparagus Cuts*
1½ cups milk
1 cup light cream
1 teaspoon salt
⅛ teaspoon pepper
Dash of nutmeg
2 crushed bouillon cubes
2 teaspoons chopped chives or onion, or 1 medium scallion or shallot, sliced
Parsley

* Or use 1 package (10 ounces) Birds Eye Chopped Spinach, Chopped Broccoli, or Whole Kernel Corn. Or use 1 package (12 ounces) Birds Eye Potato Patties and reduce salt to ½ teaspoon.

Cut block of frozen vegetable into small cubes and put in electric blender. Add milk, cream, seasonings, bouillon cubes, and chives, or onion. Cover and blend thoroughly until smooth — about 1 minute. Garnish with parsley or more chopped chives. Serve at once. To serve hot, pour soup from blender into saucepan, place over moderate heat, and bring just to a boil. Serves 4.
Note: Soup can be thinned, if desired, with additional light cream.
PREPARE-AHEAD HINT. Entire recipe may be made ahead and chilled. For hot soup, heat just before serving.

Fish bites, fish sticks, and sea scallops from the freezer make perfect appetizers for unexpected guests. Simple, too.

Quick Clam Bisque

This soup recipe calls for an electric blender and a few minutes of heating. Flavor? Enticing.

2 Birds Eye Potato Patties (½ package), thawed
1 cup milk
2 tablespoons butter
1 chicken or vegetable bouillon cube
1 can (7 ounces) minced clams
½ cup milk*
1 cup light cream

* For stronger clam flavor, use ½ cup of the clam liquor.

Break potato patties into pieces. Place potatoes, milk, butter, and bouillon cube in electric blender and blend at high speed until smooth. Drain clams and add the clams to mixture in blender. Blend at low speed 15 seconds. Pour into saucepan; stir in milk or clam juice and cream. Bring slowly to a boil, stirring constantly. Garnish with croutons or crumbled potato chips, if desired. Makes 4 cups, or 5 or 6 servings.

Italian Green Bean Antipasto

A lightly spiced appetizer, served with herring, red apple slices, onion rings, and sour cream.

1 teaspoon mixed pickling spice
1 cup water
1 package (9 ounces) Birds Eye Italian Green Beans
1 red apple, sliced
½ jar (4 ounces) herring in sour cream
Onion rings

Simmer pickling spice and water together for 10 minutes. Cool. Prepare beans as directed on package, cooking only about 1½ minutes, until tender but still crisp. Drain and cool immediately. Marinate beans in spiced liquid for at least 1 hour. Drain thoroughly.

Quick Clam Bisque (at left) is a delicate soup suited to lunches, suppers, or buffets. Note celery-leaf garnish.

Arrange beans on slices of unpeeled red apple and top with pieces of herring and sour cream sauce. Garnish with onion rings. Makes 6 antipasto servings. **PREPARE-AHEAD HINT.** Cook beans and marinate. Arrange at meal-time.

Artichoke Hearts in Marinade

Cooked artichoke hearts, thoroughly chilled in a savory dressing, for serving as first course or salad.

1 package (9 ounces) Birds Eye Artichoke Hearts
½ cup salad oil
2 tablespoons wine vinegar
1 tablespoon lemon juice
1 teaspoon salt
Dash of fresh black pepper
1 clove garlic, minced
1 teaspoon chopped chives
2 tablespoons chopped pimiento
2 tablespoons chopped green pepper
Dash of paprika

Cook artichoke hearts as directed on package. Drain. Place in bowl and chill. Meanwhile, combine remaining ingredients. Pour over chilled artichoke hearts. Let stand in refrigerator to

3

marinate at least 2 hours, stirring occasionally. Makes 4 servings.

PREPARE-AHEAD HINT. Make early in morning or night before, if desired. Flavors blend as appetizer chills.

Artichoke Antipasto

Serve chilled and flavor-blended.

2 packages (9 ounces each) Birds Eye
   Artichoke Hearts
1 cup salad oil
2 teaspoons paprika
3 tablespoons Birds Eye Concentrated
   Orange Juice
3 ounces bleu cheese
¾ teaspoon minced onion
1 teaspoon salt
Salad greens
4 hard-cooked eggs, cut in quarters

Cook artichoke hearts as directed on package. Chill. Meanwhile, combine oil, paprika, concentrated orange juice, cheese, onion, and salt. Beat until well blended. Pour over artichoke hearts. Cover and chill. Arrange salad greens and artichoke hearts on a platter or on individual plates. Garnish with egg quarters and, if desired, radishes or pimiento and parsley. Serve as antipasto. Makes 8 servings.

PREPARE-AHEAD HINT. Hard-cook eggs and refrigerate in shells. Wash salad greens and prepare other garnishes desired. Prepare artichokes and marinade; chill. Assemble antipasto at serving time.

Fish Bites Hors d'Oeuvres

An easy appetizer with a spicy dip.

1 package (8 ounces) Birds Eye
   Pre-Cooked Fish Bites
Piquant Dip

Preheat oven to 425°F. (hot). Spread frozen fish bites in shallow pan or on baking sheet. Put into hot oven and heat thoroughly until crisp — 10 to 12 minutes. Serve hot, on toothpicks, with Piquant Dip. Makes 20 hors d'oeuvres. *To Make Piquant Dip,* measure 1 tablespoon Good Seasons Onion Salad Dressing Mix (right from envelope). Blend with 1 cup sour cream, 2 tablespoons light cream, and 1 teaspoon lemon juice. Makes about 1 cup.

PREPARE-AHEAD HINT. Make dip in the morning or night before. Refrigerate. Stir before serving.

Six O'Clock Canapés

A nibble food of crackers, cheese spread, artichokes, and pimiento.

½ cup water
2 small carrots, sliced
1 small bay leaf
2 tablespoons salad oil
2 tablespoons lemon juice
1 teaspoon salt
¼ teaspoon curry powder
1 package (9 ounces) Birds Eye Artichoke
   Hearts
Crackers or Melba toast
Assorted cheese spreads or sliced cheese
Pimiento, cut in strips
Stuffed olives, sliced

Combine water, carrots, bay leaf, salad oil, lemon juice, salt, and curry powder in a medium saucepan. Simmer for 5 minutes. Add artichoke hearts, cover, and bring to a boil. Cook about 5 minutes, or until just tender. Remove from heat and cool artichoke hearts in the liquid. Drain thoroughly.

Spread crackers with assorted cheese spreads or top with a cheese slice. Place an artichoke heart on each. Garnish with strips of pimiento or olive slices. Makes about 30 canapés.

PREPARE-AHEAD HINT. Cook, drain, and chill artichokes. Finish at meal-preparation time.

A simple soup takes on company airs when served in pretty tureen and nicely garnished. For other garnishes, see ps. 1, 2.

Party Dip

You have to taste this dip to appreciate it. Excellent for graduation teas or engagement buffet.

1 package (10 ounces) Birds Eye
    Baby Lima Beans
½ teaspoon salt
¾ cup boiling water
1 package (3 ounces) cream cheese
1 cup sour cream
1 tablespoon grated onion
1 teaspoon lemon juice
4 drops Tabasco sauce
¼ teaspoon salt
Dash of pepper
3 slices crisp bacon, crumbled

Place Lima beans and ½ teaspoon salt in ¾ cup boiling water in saucepan. Bring to a boil, cover, and cook 20 minutes. Drain. Press through a ricer or blend in an electric blender. Blend in cheese until mixture is smooth. Add remaining ingredients except bacon. Chill. Sprinkle with crumbled bacon before serving. Serve with potato chips or crackers. Makes 2 cups.

Note: If desired, crumble bacon finely and mix into dip before chilling. Sprinkle with sieved hard-cooked egg and finely chopped parsley.

PREPARE-AHEAD HINT. Make dip and chill. Fry bacon, drain, and crumble just before serving.

5

Pickabacks

Colorful appetizers, quickly fixed, for planned or spur-of-the-moment parties.

Prepare 1 package (8 ounces) Birds Eye Pre-cooked Fish Bites and 1 package (8 ounces) Birds Eye Pre-cooked Fish Sticks as directed on packages. Cut fish sticks in half. Arrange fish bites and fish stick halves on toothpicks with any of the following: Stuffed olives, cocktail onions and pimiento pieces, Mandarin orange slices, pineapple chunks, or cheese slices and green pepper pieces. Keep hot for serving in chafing dish or electric skillet, if desired. Makes 30.

Chicken Liver Paté

A fashionable first course for company meals or a piquant canapé.

1 package (8 ounces) Birds Eye Frying
   Chicken Livers, thawed
½ cup butter, softened
1 tablespoon minced onion
1 teaspoon dry mustard
¾ teaspoon salt
¼ teaspoon nutmeg
Dash of cayenne

Place thawed chicken livers in a saucepan and cover with water. Then cover pan and simmer livers 15 to 20 minutes, or until tender. Drain. Press through coarse sieve. Add remaining ingredients and mix well. For appetizer, serve mounds on individual plates, garnished with crisp lettuce and tomato wedges and sprinkled with sieved hard-cooked egg. For canapé, spread on toast rounds or crisp crackers. Makes 1 cup, or 4 to 6 first-course servings. *Two-Tone Paté.* Make double the recipe for Chicken Liver Paté. Pack into one side of a 1-quart bowl that has been rubbed with oil. Cover; chill.
   Meanwhile, combine ½ cup soft butter, 1 tablespoon minced onion, 1 teaspoon dry mustard, 2 cans (4½ ounces each) deviled ham — about 1 cup; 1 hard-cooked egg, finely chopped; and ¼ to ½ teaspoon curry powder. Mix well. Pack into second half of bowl. Chill until mixtures are firm — 4 to 5 hours. Unmold. Garnish with salad greens. Makes about 10 servings. **PREPARE-AHEAD HINT.** Paté may be made a day or two in advance. Keep in covered dish in refrigerator. Allow to stand at room temperature about 1 hour to soften before using.

Spinach Hors d'Oeuvre Spread

An unusual spread of deviled ham mixed with chopped spinach and olives and prepared horse-radish.

1 package (10 ounces) Birds Eye
   Chopped Spinach, cooked
1 can (4½ ounces) deviled ham
2 teaspoons prepared horse-radish
¼ teaspoon salt
Dash of pepper
½ teaspoon lemon juice
¼ cup chopped stuffed olives
2 hard-cooked egg yolks, sieved

Combine all ingredients, except egg yolks, in small bowl. Chill. Mound in glass dish and top with sieved egg yolks. Serve as spread for assorted cocktail crackers. Makes 1⅓ cups. **PREPARE-AHEAD HINT.** Make entire recipe ahead of serving time and chill.

Hors d'Oeuvre en Brochette

Potato puffs and scallops, arranged on skewers with other tasty tidbits. Easy and elegant.

Prepare 2 packages (7 ounces each) Birds Eye Pre-cooked Sea Scallops and 1 package (8 ounces) Birds Eye Potato Puffs as directed on packages.
   Arrange on skewers, alternating the

scallops and potato puffs with pimiento strips, onion or green pepper slices, broiled mushrooms, Mandarin orange slices, or pineapple chunks. Keep hot for serving on hibachi or outdoor grill, if desired. Makes 12 to 14.

The party's off to a gracious start with potato puffs and pine-apple chunks on dainty skewers. Serve with a favorite dip.

This proud display features Supper Pie (p. 23), Angel Pudding (p. 65), Chicken-Vegetable Casserole (p. 18), Peach Chutney (p. 89), and Creamed Dried Beef with Vegetable (p. 13). Frozen strawberries and peaches garnish cream puff at lower right.

SECTION 2

GENERAL FOODS
KITCHENS

Entrées

When you plan a meal, where do you begin? With the entrée, as a rule, for two reasons: The main course is usually the most expensive part of the meal and often depends on the best buy at the market. Once chosen, the entrée dictates the rest of the menu.

A roast or ham should be balanced with lighter foods — a fruit-juice appetizer, crisp salad, and a delicate snow whip dessert, for instance. Thick soups and rich puddings or pies, on the other hand, are better suited to buffet salads, soufflés, or a vegetable plate.

These entrées from General Foods Kitchens fit into varied menus. Note that recipes have *prepare-ahead hints* to save precious minutes at the dinner hour.

GARNISHES

Surround a roast, meat loaf, chops, or fish with:
   Cooked frozen peas, Lima beans, mixed vegetables, or green beans; spiced apples; spiced
   peaches; radish roses; tomato wedges; baked
   onions; whole broiled mushrooms; green pepper
   rings; frozen French fried onion rings; or mashed
   potatoes, piped through a pastry tube around
   rim of serving platter and sprinkled with paprika, chopped parsley, or chive.

9

ACCOMPANIMENTS

For entrées: Jelly, jam, watermelon pickle, bread-and-butter pickle, spicy relish, celery, olives, or carrot curls.

Meal-in-One Supper Dish

A sausage-and-green-bean concoction, topped with a mushroom sauce.

8 link sausages (about ½ pound)
1 can (3 ounces) sliced mushrooms, drained
4 teaspoons flour
1 teaspoon salt
Dash of pepper
1¼ cups milk
¼ cup grated Parmesan cheese
3 to 4 drops Worcestershire sauce
½ medium onion, sliced into thin rings
1 tablespoon butter
2 tablespoons water
1 package (9 ounces) Birds Eye French Style Green Beans
2 small tomatoes, quartered
Melted butter

Sauté sausages until tender. Remove from skillet and keep hot.

Pour off drippings, measuring 3 tablespoons into skillet. Sauté mushrooms in drippings. Add flour, ½ teaspoon of the salt, and the pepper, blending until smooth. Then gradually add milk, stirring constantly. Add cheese and Worcestershire sauce. Cook and stir over medium heat until mixture is thickened.

Sauté onion slices in butter. Add water, remaining ½ teaspoon salt, and the green beans. Cover and bring quickly to a boil over high heat, separating beans with fork to hasten thawing, if necessary. Then reduce heat to medium and cook gently until just tender, stirring occasionally. During the cooking, add small amount of water, if needed to prevent sticking.

Meanwhile, season tomato wedges, brush with melted butter, and broil 2 to 3 minutes, or until done.

Arrange beans around the edge of a hot platter. Alternate sausage links and tomato wedges in center. Serve sauce in separate bowl to be spooned over beans, sausages, and tomatoes. Serves 4.

PREPARE-AHEAD HINT. Sauce may be prepared ahead with butter instead of sausage drippings and reheated at serving time. The sauce made with butter has a slightly different flavor.

Tangerine-Glazed Frankfurters

Here are frankfurters-with-company-manners that the teen-age cook may enjoy fixing. Serve with winter squash, coleslaw, and a savory vegetable.

1 can water
1 can (6 ounces) Birds Eye Concentrated Tangerine Juice
4 teaspoons cornstarch
¼ to ⅓ cup firmly packed light brown sugar
¼ to ½ teaspoon dry mustard
2 tablespoons Worcestershire sauce
¼ teaspoon ground cloves
¼ cup pickle relish
2 pounds frankfurters

Add 1 can water to the concentrated tangerine juice. Mix cornstarch and sugar together. Then combine all ingredients except frankfurters in a skillet. Cook until mixture thickens, about 5 to 10 minutes. Add frankfurters and cook 10 minutes longer, or until frankfurters are glazed with sauce. Serves 6.

Grape-Glazed Frankfurters. Follow above recipe, but substitute 1 can (6 ounces) Birds Eye Concentrated Grape Juice for the tangerine juice; omit pickle relish and add 1 tablespoon vinegar.

PREPARE-AHEAD HINT. Combine ingredients for glaze but do not cook until meal-preparation time.

Frankfurter Meal-in-One

Makes about 45 servings for community suppers or big family gatherings with all the aunts, uncles, and cousins.

4 packages (8 ounces each) Minute
    Sliced Potatoes
3 packages (9 ounces each) Birds Eye
    Cut Green Beans
3 quarts milk (about)
1 quart chopped onions
1 cup chopped green peppers
1 cup butter or margarine
2 cups flour
2 teaspoons salt
5 pounds frankfurters (about 50),
    cut in thirds
1 pound sharp Cheddar cheese, grated

Cook sliced potatoes as directed on packages. Cook green beans as directed on packages. Drain, measure liquid, and add enough milk to make 3 quarts.

Sauté onions and green peppers in butter or margarine until tender — about 5 minutes. Blend in flour and salt. Gradually blend in liquid. Cook, stirring constantly, until mixture is thickened. Carefully stir in potatoes and green beans. Arrange layers of vegetable mixture with the frankfurters in three 13x9x2-inch pans or four 8x8x2-inch or other shallow pans. Sprinkle with grated cheese. Bake in moderate oven (350°F.) about 30 minutes, or until mixture is bubbly and cheese is melted and lightly browned. Serves 45.

PREPARE-AHEAD HINT. Make sauce as directed, using 3 quarts of milk and omitting vegetable liquid. Refrigerate. Grate cheese and wrap in foil or cover tightly. Cut frankfurters and refrigerate. At meal-preparation time, cook vegetables, assemble casserole, and bake.

Short Ribs Supreme

A meal-in-one dish of tender, well-flavored beef short ribs, onions, potatoes, and Italian green beans.

2 tablespoons flour
1 teaspoon salt
3 pounds short ribs of beef, cut into
    serving pieces
½ cup coarsely chopped onions
⅛ teaspoon pepper
2 bay leaves
Pinch of thyme
2 tablespoons chopped parsley
3 tablespoons Birds Eye Concentrated
    Grape Juice
1 beef bouillon cube
1 cup boiling water
8 small fresh or canned white onions
8 small uncooked potatoes
1 package (9 ounces) Birds Eye Italian
    Green Beans

Combine flour and salt. Roll short rib pieces in flour mixture. Brown meat in ungreased skillet over low heat. When meat is well browned, place in 2-quart casserole or Dutch oven with a tight-fitting cover.

Add onions, pepper, bay leaves, thyme, parsley, and concentrated grape juice. Dissolve bouillon cube in the boiling water and pour into casserole. Cover and bake in slow oven (325°F.) about 2½ hours, or until meat is tender, adding hot water occasionally to prevent meat from sticking to pan.

Remove meat and skim fat from gravy. Return meat to casserole and add onions and potatoes. Cook until vegetables are tender. Cook Italian green beans as directed on package. Season to taste. Add butter, if desired. Arrange short ribs on serving platter surrounded with vegetables. Makes 4 to 6 servings. *Note:* Recipe can also be made in elec-

11

tric skillet. Brown meat at high setting. Reduce heat to simmer and cook meat with other ingredients as directed.

PREPARE-AHEAD HINT. Cook meat with seasonings 2½ hours as directed. Finish recipe at meal-preparation time.

Beef Stew Supreme

A gourmet stew made with all sorts of wonderful things, including concentrated fruit juices.

2 pounds lean beef, boned and cut in
   1½-inch cubes
½ teaspoon monosodium glutamate
1½ teaspoons salt
⅛ teaspoon pepper
3 tablespoons butter
⅓ cup diced carrots
1 cup diced onions
2 tablespoons flour
1 clove garlic, sliced
Pinch of thyme
1 bay leaf
2 tablespoons chopped parsley
2 tablespoons Birds Eye Concentrated
   Concord Grape Juice or Orange and
   Grapefruit Juice, partly thawed
1 cup beef bouillon
1 cup water
10 small white onions
10 small carrots, cut in pieces
¼ pound small fresh mushrooms, stemmed

Sprinkle meat with monosodium glutamate, salt, and pepper. Allow to stand about 20 minutes. Melt 2 tablespoons of the butter in a saucepan. Add meat, a few cubes at a time, and brown thoroughly. Add diced vegetables and brown with meat. Mix in flour, garlic, thyme, bay leaf, and parsley. Add concentrate, bouillon, and water and stir well. Cover and simmer about 1 hour, or until meat is nearly tender.

Meanwhile, brown whole onions and carrots in the remaining 1 tablespoon of butter. Remove from pan and sauté mushroom stems and caps. Add carrots

and onions to nearly tender meat; cover and cook 30 minutes. Add mushrooms and cook 15 minutes longer, or until vegetables are done. Sprinkle with parsley, if desired. Makes 8 servings.

PREPARE-AHEAD HINT. Make stew and simmer about 1 hour as directed. Cook remaining 45 minutes with vegetables at meal-preparation time.

Ham and Green Bean Rolls

Green beans rolled in ham slices and baked with a cheese sauce, topped with slivered almonds.

1 package (9 ounces) Birds Eye Whole
   Green Beans*
6 thin slices pre-cooked ham
2 tablespoons (about) prepared mustard
2 tablespoons butter
2 tablespoons flour
½ teaspoon salt
⅛ teaspoon pepper
1½ cups milk
½ cup grated Cheddar cheese
Blanched slivered almonds (optional)

* Or use 1 package (9 ounces) Birds Eye Cut Green Beans.

Cook green beans as directed on package. Drain. Divide into six portions. Spread each slice of ham lightly with mustard; roll up a portion of the beans in each ham slice. Arrange rolls in a shallow 6x10-inch baking dish.

Meanwhile, melt butter in a saucepan. Blend in flour and seasonings. Gradually add milk, stirring until well blended. Cook over low heat until thickened and smooth, stirring constantly. Add grated cheese and stir until blended. Pour over ham rolls and sprinkle with almonds, if desired. Bake in a moderate oven (375°F.) until hot and bubbly. Makes 3 servings.

PREPARE-AHEAD HINT. Make cheese sauce and sliver almonds. At meal-preparation time, fix ham rolls, cover with cheese sauce, sprinkle with almonds, and bake as directed.

Creamed Dried Beef with Vegetables

Here's a convenient recipe to keep in mind for busy days or late suppers.

1 package (10 ounces) Birds Eye
  Green Peas or Baby Lima Beans
1 can (4 ounces) sliced mushrooms,
  drained
¼ teaspoon grated onion
3 tablespoons butter
3 tablespoons flour
½ cup mushroom liquor
1 cup light cream or milk
Dash of pepper
Dash of nutmeg
1 jar (2½ ounces) dried beef

Cook peas as directed on package. Drain. Sauté mushrooms and onion in butter. Blend in flour. Combine mushroom liquor and cream and gradually blend into flour mixture, stirring constantly. Cook and stir over medium heat until thickened. Add pepper, nutmeg, cooked peas, and dried beef; heat thoroughly. Serve on toast or in patty shells. Makes 4 servings.

PREPARE-AHEAD HINT. Make sauce with seasonings as directed but omit peas and dried beef. At meal-preparation time, cook and drain peas and add with the dried beef to the sauce. Reheat.

Hamburgers Piquant

Suggested menu: Potato puffs or patties, jellied fruit-and-celery salad, hot rolls, and Hamburgers Piquant.

1 package (10 ounces) Birds Eye Mixed
  Garden Vegetables
1 pound ground beef
1½ teaspoons salt
Pepper
2 tablespoons butter
2 tablespoons flour
1¼ cups hot water
2 to 3 teaspoons horse-radish

Cook vegetables as directed on package. Drain. Season meat with 1 teaspoon salt and the pepper to taste. Shape into 4 patties. Fry patties in butter over medium heat until done as desired. Remove to warm platter. Add flour to pan drippings and stir briskly to blend. Gradually blend in water; then cook and stir until thickened. Add remaining salt, pepper to taste, cooked vegetables, and horse-radish. Stir to blend. Cook until vegetables are heated through. Pour over patties and serve immediately. Makes 2 to 4 servings.

Spinach-Stuffed Ham Slices

Two ham slices baked sandwich-fashion with a spinach filling and served with a pungent sauce.

1 package (10 ounces) Birds Eye
  Chopped Spinach
¼ cup diced celery
1 can (4 ounces) chopped mushrooms,
  drained — about ½ cup
2 tablespoons chopped onion
2 tablespoons salad oil
¼ teaspoon salt
⅛ teaspoon pepper
2 slices (½ pound each) pre-cooked ham,
  ¼ to ½ inch thick
1 tablespoon butter, melted
Horse-Radish Cream Sauce (p. 14)

Cook spinach as directed on package. Drain. Sauté celery, mushrooms, and onion in salad oil over medium heat until celery and onion are transparent. Add to spinach. Add salt and pepper.

Place one ham slice in a shallow baking dish. Spread with spinach mixture. Top with remaining ham slice. Brush with melted butter. Cover and bake in a moderate oven (350°F.) for 15 minutes. Uncover and continue baking until lightly browned — about 15 minutes. Serve with Horse-Radish Cream Sauce. Makes 4 or 5 servings.

To make **Horse-Radish Cream Sauce,**
melt 2 tablespoons butter in a small
saucepan. Blend in 2 tablespoons flour,
¼ teaspoon salt, and dash of pepper.
Gradually add 1¼ cups milk, stirring
constantly. Cook and stir over medium
heat until sauce is thickened and
smooth. Stir in ¼ cup prepared horse-
radish. Serve hot. Makes 1⅓ cups.
PREPARE-AHEAD HINT. Prepare stuffing and Horse-Radish Cream Sauce.
Reheat stuffing slightly before spreading
on ham. Reheat sauce before serving.

Patio Meat Balls

*An easy supper dish with meat balls
and vegetables in gravy. Serve with a
jellied salad such as Strawberry-Grapefruit Chill (p. 47).*

3 slices day-old bread
1 pound ground beef*
1 tablespoon minced onion
1 egg
1 teaspoon salt
Dash of pepper
½ teaspoon fennel seed (optional)
1 tablespoon butter
1 can (8 ounces) tomato sauce
1 package (10 ounces) Birds Eye
   Green Peas
1 package (10 ounces) Birds Eye
   Succotash

* Or use 1 pound bulk sausage and omit bread,
onion, egg, salt, pepper, and butter.

Soak bread in water to cover until soft,
squeeze dry, and break into crumbs.
Mix bread, ground beef, onion, egg,
salt, pepper, and fennel in a bowl. Form
into 1-inch balls. Brown meat balls in
butter. Then add tomato sauce, cover,
and simmer 15 minutes. Meanwhile,
cook vegetables according to package
directions. Then add to meat balls. Stir
and serve. Makes 4 to 6 servings.
PREPARE-AHEAD HINT. Make meat
mixture, form into balls, and refrigerate. At meal-preparation time, proceed
with recipe as directed.

Glazed Ham

*Perfect with baked sweet potato, as-
paragus spears, and celery strips.*

½ pre-cooked ham, about 7 pounds
Whole cloves
1 can (6 ounces) Birds Eye Concentrated
   Orange Juice, thawed*
¼ cup firmly packed brown sugar
Pinch of ground clove
Pinch of ground cinnamon

* Or use Birds Eye Concentrated Lemonade,
Limeade, Orange and Grapefruit Juice, Grapefruit, or Tangerine Juice.

Place ham, fat side up, on rack in
shallow pan; (do not cover or add
water). Insert meat thermometer. Bake
in slow oven (325°F.) about 1½ hours.
Then remove from oven and pour fat
drippings from pan. Score ham fat, cutting only ¼ inch deep. Dot with whole
cloves. Mix together thawed concentrated orange juice, brown sugar, and
spices. Pour about half of mixture over
ham; return to oven. Bake another 30
minutes, or until meat thermometer reg-
isters 130°F., basting with remaining
orange juice mixture occasionally. Remove ham to hot platter. Pour off
grease from pan. Add enough water to
pan to give glaze a sauce consistency.
Bring to a boil and serve with ham.
Makes about 12 servings.

Glazed Pork Roast

*Pork roast glazed with tangerine con-
centrate and brown sugar and served
with spiced crab apples.*

6 to 7 pounds pork roast
1 can (6 ounces) Birds Eye Concentrated
   Tangerine Juice, thawed
¼ to ⅓ cup firmly packed brown sugar
2 jars (1 pound each) spiced crab
   apples (optional)

Wipe roast with a damp cloth. Place
on a rack in a shallow roasting pan. (If
desired, insert a meat thermometer in
the lean part of a meaty rib.)

Roast in moderate oven (350°F.) for about 4 to 4½ hours. Mix tangerine juice with brown sugar. Baste roast with a third of the mixture. Then continue roasting for about another half hour — or to a temperature of 185°F. on meat thermometer. Baste two or three times during cooking.

When roast is done, place on a heated platter and let stand about 20 minutes for easier carving. Meanwhile, heat crab apples and juice in a saucepan. Arrange apples around roast. Pour off grease from baking pan. Add enough water to pan to give glaze a sauce consistency. Bring to a boil and serve with the meat. Makes 10 to 12 servings.

Note: If desired, have butcher prepare pork as a crown roast. Cover rib ends with aluminum foil during roasting. Remove foil before serving roast and fill center of crown with crab apples.

PREPARE-AHEAD HINT. Mix fruit juice and brown sugar, if desired, and refrigerate. Cover rib ends of crown roast, if used, with aluminum foil ready for roasting.

Artichokes Benedict

An open-faced sandwich, topped with hollandaise sauce, for luncheon or supper, or Sunday brunch.

2 egg yolks
¼ cup butter, melted
¼ cup boiling water
2 teaspoons lemon juice
¼ teaspoon salt
Dash of pepper
Dash of cayenne pepper
1 package (9 ounces) Birds Eye Artichoke Hearts
4 thin slices boiled ham
1 tablespoon butter
2 English muffins, split and toasted

Beat egg yolks until thick and lemon-colored. Add melted butter gradually, beating constantly. Add boiling water slowly, beating after each addition. Cook and stir over hot water until thickened. Remove from heat. Add lemon juice, salt, pepper, and cayenne.

Cook artichokes as directed on the package. Sauté ham in butter until browned. Arrange ham on toasted muffin halves. Top with artichokes and sauce. Makes 4 servings.

Sweet-Sour Spareribs and Beans

Try with coleslaw and hashed brown or baked potatoes.

3 pounds spareribs, cut in serving pieces
1 can (6 ounces) Birds Eye Concentrated Lemonade
2 cans water
3 tablespoons soy sauce
½ teaspoon salt
3 tablespoons catsup
1 to 2 teaspoons vinegar (optional)
3 tablespoons firmly packed brown sugar
1 package (9 ounces) Birds Eye Cut Wax Beans
1 can (8½ ounces) small white onions
1 small green pepper, sliced
2 tablespoons cold water
1 to 2 tablespoons cornstarch

Place spareribs in a skillet. Add just enough water to cover, bring to a boil, reduce heat, and simmer 1 hour. Pour off water.

Combine lemonade concentrate and the 2 cans of water. Add soy sauce, salt, catsup, vinegar, and brown sugar. Pour ⅔ cup mixture over ribs, cover, and cook 1 hour over medium heat, or until tender. Add more of the concentrated mixture, if necessary.

Cook wax beans as directed on package, adding the onions with the beans. Drain. Arrange with spareribs on hot platter. Garnish with green pepper.

Pour off excess fat from skillet. Add remaining sauce. Blend cold water into cornstarch. Then stir into sauce in skillet. Cook, stirring constantly, until sauce is thickened and smooth. If sauce appears too thick, thin with about ¼ cup hot water. Serve separately to be poured over meat and vegetables, if desired. Makes 3 or 4 servings.

PREPARE-AHEAD HINT. Simmer spareribs 1 hour. Combine ingredients for concentrate mixture and refrigerate. Then at meal-preparation time, place spareribs in skillet, cover with ⅔ cup concentrate mixture; cook wax beans with onions, and proceed as directed.

Braised Breast of Lamb

A thrifty oven dish of well-flavored lamb, served with a vegetable gravy.

2 to 2½ pounds breast of lamb
2 tablespoons flour
1½ teaspoons salt
¼ teaspoon pepper
1 cup water
1 cup chopped onions
2 small bay leaves
1 clove garlic (optional)
1 cup celery strips
1 package (10 ounces) Birds Eye Peas
  and Carrots

Trim excess fat and backbone from lamb breasts so that they lie flat. Rub with flour and place in Dutch oven or roasting pan. Brown well under broiler. (Or brown well in a skillet over medium heat, if desired.) Sprinkle with salt and pepper. Add water, onions, bay leaves, garlic, and celery. Cover. Bake in slow oven (325°F.) about 2 hours, or until very tender. Add more hot water during cooking, if necessary.

Meanwhile, cook peas and carrots as directed on package. Remove lamb breasts to hot platter. Add vegetables to gravy in roasting pan and pour over meat. Makes 4 servings.

PREPARE-AHEAD HINT. Trim meat and brown as directed. Blend the 1 cup water (called for in recipe) with the drippings in pan or skillet. Refrigerate water mixture and meat. At meal-preparation time, season meat, add bay leaves, onions, and celery and proceed with recipe as directed.

Lamb and Green Bean Stew

Try with a salad of mixed greens, avocado slices, and grapefruit sections; bread sticks, and condiments.

1 pound stewing lamb, cubed
½ cup sliced onions
2 tablespoons butter or other fat
¾ cup water
1½ cups canned tomatoes
1½ cups diced potatoes
1 package (9 ounces) Birds Eye Cut
  Green Beans
1½ teaspoons salt
¼ teaspoon pepper
1 teaspoon Worcestershire sauce
¼ cup cold water
2 tablespoons flour

Brown lamb and onions in the fat. Add ¾ cup water, cover, and simmer 1½ hours, or until meat is nearly tender. Add tomatoes, potatoes, frozen green beans, salt, pepper, and Worcestershire sauce, and cook 25 minutes, or until vegetables are done. Gradually blend ¼ cup water with the flour, stirring until smooth. Add to stew, stirring vigorously, until mixture comes to a boil. Simmer 5 minutes longer, or until gravy is slightly thickened. Pour into heated casserole and garnish with parsley sprigs, if desired. Serves 5 or 6.

Saucepan Stew. Prepare Lamb and Green Bean Stew, browning lamb and onions in an electric saucepan set at 350°F. Reduce heat to 200°F. and continue as directed.

PREPARE-AHEAD HINT. Simmer meat with onions 1½ hours as directed. At meal-preparation time, add vegetables and finish cooking.

Orange-Glazed Lamb Chops with Onions

Here's a simple and flavorful way to dress up chops, chicken, or ham.

8 lamb chops
Salt and pepper
2 tablespoons butter
2 dozen canned or parboiled small white onions
1 can (6 ounces) Birds Eye Concentrated Orange Juice, thawed

Sprinkle lamb chops with salt and pepper. Fry in butter in skillet until browned on both sides. Arrange chops and onions in a roasting pan. Stir concentrated juice into drippings in skillet; then pour over meat. Cover and bake in moderate oven (350°F.) for 30 minutes. Remove cover. Continue baking, basting frequently until meat is tender — about 15 minutes. Makes 8 servings.

Orange-Glazed Pork Chops with Onions. Use above recipe, but substitute pork chops for the lamb chops.

Orange-Glazed Broilers with Onions. Use above recipe, but substitute 2 quartered broiling chickens (2 pounds each) for the lamb chops. Serves 4.

Orange-Glazed Ham Slices with Onions. Use above recipe, but substitute 2 center cut ham slices (¾ inch thick) for the lamb chops.

PREPARE-AHEAD HINT. If you use raw onions in this recipe, remove the outer skins and boil onions in water to cover just until they are barely tender.

Veal Roulades

Rolled veal cutlets, with a savory spinach stuffing.

Spinach Stuffing (p. 78)
6 thinly sliced veal cutlets
2 tablespoons salad oil
1 can (10½ ounces) condensed cream of mushroom soup
¼ cup water

Make Spinach Stuffing as directed. Spread each cutlet with 1 heaping tablespoon. Roll as for jelly roll and turn ends; fasten with toothpicks. Brown slowly in salad oil over medium heat. Combine mushroom soup and water. Pour over cutlets. Cover and simmer 1 hour, or until tender. Serves 3.

PREPARE-AHEAD HINT. Make stuffing and fix cutlet rolls, ready to cook.

Swiss Veal with Limas

Serve with creamed potatoes and an endive-orange salad.

¼ cup flour
1 teaspoon salt
⅛ teaspoon pepper
1½ pounds veal steak, 1 inch thick
2 tablespoons shortening or oil
2 cups sliced onions
⅔ cup slivered green pepper
¾ cup tomato juice
¼ teaspoon basil
1 package (10 ounces) Birds Eye Baby Lima Beans, Fordhook Lima Beans, or Butter Beans, partly thawed
½ teaspoon salt

Combine flour, 1 teaspoon salt, and the pepper and pound mixture into the veal. Reserve any remaining flour mixture. Melt shortening in a skillet over medium-high heat. Sauté veal in shortening until well browned on both sides. Remove meat from skillet and add onions and green pepper. Sauté, stirring to coat vegetables with drippings. Add remaining flour mixture and blend. Gradually stir in tomato juice and basil; then return meat to skillet and baste with sauce. Cover and simmer 45 minutes over low heat. Arrange Limas around veal, sprinkle with ½ teaspoon salt, and cook, covered, about 30 minutes longer, or until beans and meat are tender. Makes about 4 servings.

Note: When cooking in electric skillet,

set at 350°F. for medium-high heat and 200°F. for low heat.

PREPARE-AHEAD HINT. Prepare veal and simmer 45 minutes as directed. Finish cooking with the Lima beans at meal-preparation time.

Chicken and Vegetables in Cream

Serve with rice, a jellied fruit salad, and spice cake squares topped with Lemon Sauce (p. 81).

1 Birds Eye Frying Chicken, partly thawed
½ cup flour
2 teaspoons salt
¼ teaspoon pepper
Dash of cayenne
¼ cup butter, margarine, or shortening
1 cup water
2 packages (10 ounces each) Birds Eye Succotash, partly thawed*
1 cup chopped onions
1 cup light cream
1 teaspoon salt

* If desired, use 1 package (10 ounces) Birds Eye Whole Kernel Corn and 1 package (10 ounces) Birds Eye Fordhook Lima Beans instead of the succotash.

Separate pieces of chicken. Dry between towels. Combine flour, 2 teaspoons salt, the pepper, and cayenne. Roll chicken in the seasoned flour. (Or shake chicken and flour in paper bag.)

Heat fat in skillet. Fry chicken until very brown but not tender, turning occasionally. Then add water and the chicken gizzard, cut in small pieces. Cover and simmer until chicken is almost tender — about 25 minutes.

Add succotash, onions, cream, 1 teaspoon salt, and the chicken liver, cut in small pieces. Cover and cook over medium heat until chicken and vegetables are tender — about 15 minutes. To serve, arrange chicken on plate and spoon vegetables and cream sauce over the top. Makes 4 servings.

PREPARE-AHEAD HINT. Brown chicken and cook about 25 minutes as directed.

At meal-preparation time, add rest of ingredients and finish cooking.

Chicken-Vegetable Casserole

General Foods Kitchens developed this recipe with community suppers in mind. But the casserole is also excellent for feeding a crowd of hungry teenagers.

5 packages (10 ounces each) Birds Eye Chopped Broccoli or Green Peas
1½ cups (¾ pound) chicken fat or butter
2 cups sifted flour
3 tablespoons salt
½ teaspoon pepper
2½ quarts milk
1¼ quarts chicken stock*
½ cup finely chopped onions
3 tablespoons lemon juice
1¼ pounds spaghetti, cooked and drained
2 chickens (about 5½ pounds each), cooked and diced — about 1¾ quarts
1 pound Cheddar cheese, grated

* Or use 6 chicken bouillon cubes dissolved in 1¼ quarts boiling water.

Cook broccoli as directed on the package. Drain. Meanwhile, melt chicken fat in top of a large double boiler. Stir in flour, salt, and pepper. Gradually stir in milk and chicken stock, blending well. Add onions. Cook over boiling water, stirring occasionally, until mixture is thickened. Add broccoli, lemon juice, cooked spaghetti, and chicken. Mix well. Pour into five 8x8x2-inch baking pans, or three 9x13x2-inch baking dishes, or two 11x17x3-inch roasting pans. Sprinkle with cheese. Bake in moderate oven (350°F.) about 30 minutes, or until bubbly and heated through. Then place under broiler until cheese is lightly browned. Makes 30 servings, about 1 cup each.

Turkey-Vegetable Casserole. Use the above recipe but substitute an 8- to 9-pound turkey, cooked and diced — about 1¾ cups — for the chicken.

PREPARE-AHEAD HINT. Cook poultry, remove skin, and dice poultry meat. Cook spaghetti and make sauce. Grate cheese and wrap in foil. At meal-preparation time, cook vegetables, assemble casserole and bake as directed, allowing at least 10 minutes more than the time called for in recipe.

Chicken, South German Style

Chicken coated with an egg-bread-and-cheese mixture; then fried and served with a mushroom sauce.

1 Birds Eye Frying Chicken, thawed
Flour
Salt
Pepper
2 eggs
¼ cup water
½ cup fine soft bread crumbs
½ cup grated Parmesan cheese
⅓ cup butter or other fat
Mushroom Sauce

Separate pieces of chicken and dry between towels. Combine flour, salt, and pepper and roll chicken in seasoned flour. Or shake chicken and flour in a paper bag. Combine eggs and water and beat well. Combine bread crumbs and Parmesan cheese. Dip chicken in egg mixture, then roll in crumb-cheese mixture. Sauté slowly in fat over low heat about 45 minutes, or until tender. Serve with Mushroom Sauce. Serves 4. *To make* **Mushroom Sauce,** chop ½ pound fresh mushrooms and sauté in ¼ cup butter until tender. Blend in 2 tablespoons flour, ½ teaspoon salt, and dash of pepper; stir until smooth. Gradually add 1 cup milk, stirring constantly. Cook and stir over medium heat until mixture is thickened. Then stir in 1 tablespoon lemon juice. Serve hot.
PREPARE-AHEAD HINT. Make sauce ahead of time, omitting lemon juice; before serving, reheat sauce and then add the lemon juice.

Precisely right for Sunday supper or Tuesday bridge are Artichokes Benedict (p. 15). And so easy for the hostess.

Artichoke Casserole Poulet

A truly gourmet dish that uses left-over chicken.

1 package (9 ounces) Birds Eye Artichoke Hearts
2 tablespoons butter
2 tablespoons flour
½ cup milk
½ cup chicken stock
⅓ cup grated cheese
Salt and pepper to taste
1½ cups cooked chicken, cut in bite-size pieces

Cook artichokes as directed on the package. Melt butter in a saucepan; stir in flour, blending well. Gradually add milk and chicken stock, stirring constantly. Cook and stir until thickened and smooth.

Remove from heat and stir in 4 tablespoons of the grated cheese. Season with salt and pepper to taste. Layer artichoke hearts and chicken in a greased 1- or 1½-quart casserole, starting with artichoke hearts. Pour cheese sauce over artichokes and chicken. Sprinkle with remaining grated cheese. If desired, add a dash of paprika. Bake in moderate oven (375°F.) for 15 to 20 minutes. Makes 4 servings.
PREPARE-AHEAD HINT. Make cheese sauce and cut up chicken; refrigerate.

Chicken Cosmopolitan

Chicken breasts in a casserole with broccoli and Cheddar cheese.

2 packages (1 pound each) Birds Eye
  Frying Chicken Breasts, partly thawed
Flour, salt, pepper
¼ cup fat
1 can condensed cream of mushroom or
  celery soup
1⅓ cups water
1 package (10 ounces) Birds Eye Broccoli
  Spears or Chopped Broccoli
1 cup grated Cheddar cheese

Separate chicken pieces and dry between towels. Combine flour, salt, and pepper. Roll chicken in seasoned flour. Sauté in fat, browning all sides. Remove chicken. Combine soup and water with drippings in skillet, blending well. Return chicken to skillet, cover, and simmer until tender, about 45 minutes.

Cook broccoli as directed on package; drain and arrange in greased shallow baking dish. Remove bones from chicken and place chicken on broccoli. Cover with gravy and sprinkle with the cheese. Broil 2 to 3 minutes, or just long enough to melt cheese. Serves 4.
PREPARE-AHEAD HINT. Brown chicken and simmer 10 to 15 minutes. Finish cooking at meal-preparation time.

Liver á La Suisse

Sautéed beef liver served with an unusual gravy, flavored with grapefruit juice concentrate.

1 pound beef liver, sliced ½-inch thick
4 strips bacon
4 tablespoons flour
1 teaspoon salt
Dash of pepper
1 cup chopped onions
¾ to 1 cup hot water
1 tablespoon Birds Eye Concentrated
  Grapefruit Juice

Trim membranes and vessels from liver and dry well with paper towel. Sauté bacon in heavy saucepan until crisp. Remove bacon. Dip liver slices in 3 tablespoons of the flour, seasoned with ½ teaspoon salt and the pepper. Quickly brown liver in hot bacon fat. Reduce heat. Cover and cook until liver is tender, about 10 minutes. Remove liver to hot serving platter and keep warm. Brown onions in bacon fat. Add remaining flour, stirring constantly, until flour is well browned. Gradually add water, stirring constantly. Add remaining salt and the concentrated grapefruit juice. Heat thoroughly. Pour over liver. Sprinkle with crumbled crisp bacon. Makes 3 servings.

Smothered Chicken

Frying chicken cooked with onions and mushrooms and served with a thick cream gravy.

1 Birds Eye Frying Chicken, thawed
Flour
Salt
Pepper
¼ cup butter or other fat
½ cup chopped onions
½ pound fresh mushrooms, sliced*
¼ cup hot water
3 tablespoons flour
½ teaspoon salt
Dash of pepper
1 cup milk
½ cup light cream

* Or use 1 can (4 ounces) sliced mushrooms, drained.

Separate pieces of chicken and dry between towels. Combine flour, salt, and pepper and roll chicken in the seasoned flour. Sauté in fat in skillet until brown on all sides. Remove chicken. Brown onions and mushrooms in drippings in skillet. Return chicken to skillet and add hot water. Cover and simmer gently 30 to 45 minutes, or until tender. Remove chicken to hot platter and keep warm for serving.

Stir flour, ½ teaspoon salt, and dash of pepper into mixture in skillet and blend well. Gradually add milk and cream, stirring constantly. Cook and stir over medium heat until gravy is thickened and smooth. Pour over the chicken. Makes 4 servings.

Fluffy Chive Omelet

Omelets and soufflés made with Minute Tapioca stay high and fluffy longer than other such egg dishes. Luscious with cheese-vegetable sauce.

2 tablespoons Minute Tapioca
¾ teaspoon salt
⅛ teaspoon pepper
¾ cup milk
1 tablespoon butter
4 egg whites
4 egg yolks
1 tablespoon finely chopped chives
Cheese-Vegetable Sauce

Combine Minute Tapioca, salt, pepper, and milk in saucepan. Place over medium heat and cook until mixture comes to a boil, stirring constantly. Add butter. Remove from heat and allow to cool slightly.

Meanwhile, beat egg whites until stiff. Beat egg yolks until thick and lemon colored. Add chives and tapioca mixture to egg yolks and mix well. Fold into egg whites.

Spoon into hot buttered 10-inch skillet. Cook over low heat 3 minutes. Then bake in moderate oven (350°F.) 15 minutes. Omelet is sufficiently cooked when a knife inserted comes out clean. Cut across at right angles to handle of pan, being careful not to cut all the way through. Fold carefully from handle to opposite side and place on hot platter. Top each serving with Cheese-Vegetable Sauce. Makes 5 or 6 servings. *To make Cheese-Vegetable Sauce,* cook 2 packages (10 ounces each) Birds

Eye Mixed Garden Vegetables as directed on package. Drain. Melt 1 tablespoon butter in medium saucepan. Blend in 2 tablespoons flour. Gradually stir in 1½ cups milk until mixture is smooth. Then cook and stir until thick. Add ¾ cup grated Cheddar cheese, ¼ to ½ teaspoon salt, and a dash of pepper. Blend. Add 2 cups of the drained vegetables. Arrange remaining vegetables around omelet on platter.

PREPARE-AHEAD HINT. Grate cheese and wrap in foil. Make white sauce and reheat at meal-preparation time. Finish sauce as directed.

Curried Chicken Livers

An excellent recipe for smorgasbord-type dinners or buffets.

3 packages (8 ounces each) Birds Eye
    Frying Chicken Livers, thawed
½ cup butter
6 tablespoons finely chopped onion
1½ cups thinly sliced mushrooms
6 tablespoons flour
1½ teaspoons curry powder
1¼ teaspoons salt
Dash of pepper
1⅓ cups chicken broth*
1⅓ cups milk

* Or dissolve 1 chicken bouillon cube in 1⅓ cups boiling water.

Dry chicken livers between paper towels. Sauté in butter in skillet about 6 minutes, stirring frequently. Remove from skillet and set aside. Add onion and mushrooms to skillet and sauté until lightly browned. Add flour and seasonings and stir until blended. Gradually add chicken broth and milk, stirring constantly. Cook and stir until mixture is thickened. Add chicken livers and heat thoroughly. Serve at once or keep warm in chafing dish or electric skillet. Serve on rice. Serves 8.

PREPARE-AHEAD HINT. Chop onion and slice mushrooms, if desired, and wrap in foil until ready to use.

Broccoli Grill

A glorified open-faced sandwich of broccoli, bacon, cheese, and tomato, lightly broiled.

1 package (10 ounces) Birds Eye
　Chopped Broccoli
6 slices bacon
6 slices buttered toast
6 slices American cheese
6 slices tomato
1 tablespoon butter, melted
Salt and pepper

Cook broccoli as directed on the package. Drain and season to taste. Meanwhile, fry bacon until crisp; drain on paper toweling.

Arrange broccoli on buttered toast. Top each serving with a slice of bacon, then a slice of cheese, and a slice of tomato. Brush tomato with melted butter and sprinkle with salt and pepper. Heat under broiler about 5 minutes, or until tomato slices are lightly browned. Makes 6 servings.

Deviled Egg Casserole

Here's a dish with many uses. Perfect for meatless or vegetarian meals.

6 hard-cooked eggs
3 tablespoons mayonnaise
⅛ teaspoon dry mustard
Dash of pepper
2 packages (10 ounces each) Birds Eye
　Chopped Broccoli or Chopped Spinach
¼ cup butter
2 tablespoons flour
2 cups milk
1 cup grated sharp American cheese
½ teaspoon Worcestershire sauce
½ teaspoon salt
Dash of pepper
Dash of Tabasco sauce

Cut eggs in half lengthwise. Remove yolks and mash well. Add mayonnaise,

mustard, and dash of pepper. Blend well. Fill egg whites with yolk mixture.

Cook broccoli as directed on the package. Drain well. Meanwhile, melt butter in saucepan. Add flour and stir until blended. Then add milk gradually and cook over medium heat until mixture is thickened, stirring constantly. Set aside 2 tablespoons grated cheese. Add rest to sauce and stir until cheese is melted. Add seasonings.

Place broccoli in well-greased 1½-quart baking dish. Add half of cheese sauce, mixing sauce and broccoli with fork. Arrange eggs on top; pour remaining sauce over all. Sprinkle with the remaining 2 tablespoons cheese. Bake in moderate oven (375°F.) 20 to 25 minutes, or until bubbly and lightly browned. Makes 6 servings.

PREPARE-AHEAD HINT. Prepare entire casserole, but do not bake until meal-preparation time. Allow an extra 10 minutes for chilled casserole to heat.

Asparagus Soufflé

A soufflé that holds up well. Excellent for Sunday brunch with a fruit cup as starter and plenty of crisp bacon.

1 package (10 ounces) Birds Eye
　Asparagus Cuts
¼ cup butter or margarine
2 teaspoons grated onion
¼ cup Minute Tapioca
1½ cups milk
1 teaspoon salt
⅛ teaspoon pepper
⅛ teaspoon marjoram
½ teaspoon Worcestershire sauce
6 or 7 drops Tabasco sauce
4 egg whites
4 egg yolks

Cook asparagus as directed on package. Drain. Melt butter in saucepan. Add grated onion, Minute Tapioca, milk, salt, and pepper. Cook and stir over medium heat until mixture comes to a boil. Remove from heat and add marjoram, Worcestershire sauce, Tabasco sauce, and drained asparagus. Allow to cool slightly while beating eggs.

Beat egg whites until stiff peaks form. Beat egg yolks until thick and lemon-colored. Add tapioca mixture to egg yolks and mix well. Fold into egg whites. Spoon into 2-quart baking dish. Place in pan of hot water and bake in moderate oven (350°F.) for 1 hour and 15 minutes, or until soufflé is firm. Serve plain or with crisp bacon or a cheese sauce. Makes 6 to 8 servings.

Green Bean Rarebit with Baked Potatoes

Serve with thin slices of grilled ham and a tossed green salad.

5 baking potatoes
1 package (9 ounces) Birds Eye Cut or French Style Green Beans
Milk
2 tablespoons fat
¼ cup flour
1½ teaspoons salt
Dash of pepper
¼ teaspoon paprika
1½ teaspoons grated onion
½ to ¾ cup grated American cheese
¼ teaspoon Worcestershire sauce
1 tablespoon diced pimiento

Wash potatoes, dry, and rub skins with salad oil or margarine. Bake in hot oven (450°F.) for 45 to 60 minutes, or until done.

Cook beans as directed on package. Drain, reserving liquid; add milk to make 2 cups. Melt fat in saucepan. Stir in flour, salt, pepper, paprika, and onion, blending well. Add liquid gradually and cook until mixture is thickened and smooth, stirring constantly. Add cheese, Worcestershire sauce, beans, and pimiento; stir until cheese is melted and mixture is thoroughly heated.

Break open hot potatoes, season with salt and pepper, and arrange on platter. Cover with rarebit mixture. Serve at once. Makes 5 servings.

PREPARE-AHEAD HINT. Wash and oil potatoes, ready for baking. Make sauce, using all milk for liquid. Grate cheese and wrap in foil. At meal-preparation time, bake potatoes, cook beans, reheat sauce. Add cheese, beans, and other ingredients as directed.

Supper Pie

A cheese crust with a custard-spinach filling, flavored with onion and mushrooms. Serve large wedges with grilled Canadian bacon or pork sausage.

1 package (10 ounces) Birds Eye Chopped Spinach*
½ cup milk
½ cup light cream
½ cup finely chopped onions
¼ cup chopped mushrooms
1 teaspoon salt
¼ teaspoon nutmeg
Dash of pepper
3 eggs, slightly beaten
1 unbaked 9-inch Cheese Crust (p. 24)

* Or use 1 package (10 ounces) Birds Eye Asparagus Cuts.

Cook spinach as directed on the package. Drain well. Meanwhile, combine the milk, light cream, chopped onions, chopped mushrooms, salt, nutmeg, and pepper in a saucepan. Simmer 1 minute. Add a small amount of the hot mixture to the eggs. Blend well. Add to remaining hot mixture in saucepan and stir until well blended.

Add spinach to hot custard and mix well. Pour into 9-inch unbaked Cheese Crust. Bake in a hot oven (400°F.) 15 minutes; then reduce heat to 325°F. and bake an additional 20 to 25 minutes, or until a silver knife inserted in the center of the pie comes out clean. Makes 6 servings.

23

Cheese Crust. Combine 1 cup grated Cheddar cheese, ¾ cup flour, ½ teaspoon salt, ¼ teaspoon dry mustard, and ¼ cup melted butter, using pastry blender or fork. Mix well. Press firmly on bottom and sides of 9-inch pie pan. **PREPARE-AHEAD HINT.** Prepare crust and fit into pan. (Do not bake.) Chop onions and mushrooms and mix with milk, cream, and seasonings. Refrigerate until meal-preparation time; then cook vegetable. Simmer milk-mushroom mixture and proceed as directed.

Tuna au Gratin

Makes 18 to 24 servings for community suppers or parties.

6 packages (10 ounces each) Birds Eye
   Green Peas*
1¼ cups butter
1 cup finely chopped onions
½ cup coarsely chopped celery
¾ cup sifted flour
3 teaspoons salt
½ teaspoon pepper
2 quarts milk
4 cups water
5 cups grated sharp Cheddar cheese —
   about 1 pound
2 tablespoons lemon juice
4 cups Minute Rice
9 cans (6 to 7 ounces each) tuna fish,
   drained and flaked — about 9 cups
4 cups buttered bread cubes

* Or use 6 packages (10 ounces each) Birds Eye
Baby Lima Beans or 6 packages (9 ounces each)
Birds Eye Cut or French Style Green Beans.

Cook peas as directed on package. Drain. Melt butter in 6-quart saucepan. Add onions and celery; sauté until golden brown. Stir in flour, salt, and pepper and blend well. Then gradually add milk and water, stirring constantly. Cook and stir over medium heat until mixture is thickened. Remove from heat and blend in cheese and lemon juice.

Pour 2 cups of the cheese sauce into two 13x9x2-inch pans; then add 2 cups rice (measured right from package) to each pan. Stir. Combine tuna, peas, and remaining sauce and pour over rice. Top with bread cubes and bake in moderate oven (375°F.) about 15 minutes, or until bread cubes are browned. Makes 18 to 24 servings.

Note: Mixture may also be baked in one 20x12-inch pan or in five 8x8x2-inch ovenproof baking dishes.

Crab Meat au Gratin. Use above recipe but substitute 9 cans (6 to 7 ounces each) crab meat, drained and flaked, for the tuna fish.

Supper au Gratin. Use above recipe but substitute 9 cups of diced cooked chicken, turkey, or veal for the tuna fish and omit the lemon juice.

PREPARE-AHEAD HINT. Make sauce with onions and celery as directed but omit cheese and lemon juice. Grate cheese. Prepare bread cubes. At meal-preparation time, cook vegetables, drain and flake fish, reheat sauce, and add cheese and lemon juice. Assemble casserole and bake as directed.

Fillets with Egg-Mustard Sauce

Suggested menu: Vegetable Blender Soup, (p. 2), fillets, French fried potatoes, tomato salad, bread sticks, and a cobbler for dessert.

2 packages (12 ounces each) Birds Eye
   Cod or Haddock Fillets
Salt, pepper, and flour
¼ cup butter or other fat
2 teaspoons flour
½ teaspoon salt
Dash of pepper
1 cup milk
1 tablespoon dry mustard
1 tablespoon lemon juice
1 hard-cooked egg, finely chopped
Chopped parsley

Cut fillets in serving portions. Sprinkle

with salt and pepper; then roll in flour. Fry in butter in heavy skillet about 15 minutes, turning to brown both sides. Remove fish from skillet. Keep hot.

Add 2 teaspoons flour, ½ teaspoon salt, and dash of pepper to fat left in skillet; blend. Gradually stir in milk. Cook over medium heat until mixture is thickened, stirring constantly. Blend mustard and lemon juice together. Stir into sauce. Add egg. Serve hot over fish. Garnish with chopped parsley. Makes 3 to 5 servings.

PREPARE-AHEAD HINT. Hard-cook egg and refrigerate in shell. Chop parsley and wrap in foil until ready to use.

Feast for a hungry family — Glazed Pork Roast (p. 14) — 'does any cook proud.' For convenience, serve with oven-baked foods.

Broiled Fish with Cucumber Sauce

Here's an incomparable fish sauce of cucumber, parsley, and seasonings, intended for connoisseurs.

2 packages (12 ounces each) Birds Eye
    Flounder, Cod, or Haddock Fillets,
    partly thawed
Cucumber Sauce

Broil fish as directed on package. Remove to hot platter and pour Cucumber Sauce over the hot fish. Serves 4 to 6.

*To make **Cucumber Sauce**,* melt ¼ cup butter in a saucepan. Add 1 teaspoon vinegar, 1 tablespoon lemon juice, ½ teaspoon grated onion, dash of salt, dash of pepper, and 4 drops Tabasco sauce. Stir to blend well. Then remove from heat and add 3 tablespoons grated cucumber and 2 tablespoons chopped parsley or chives.

PREPARE-AHEAD HINT. Make sauce, omitting cucumber and parsley. At serving time, reheat sauce and add the grated cucumber and chopped parsley.

North, south, east, west, ham's best when checkered, spiked with cloves, burnished with fruit-juice glaze. Recipe on p. 14.

Shrimp Wiggle

Shrimp and peas in a well-flavored white sauce. Serve on toasted English muffin halves, toast, or crackers.

1 package (10 ounces) Birds Eye
  Green Peas
2 packages (7 ounces each) frozen
  shrimp*
¼ cup butter
¼ cup flour
2 cups milk
¾ teaspoon salt
Dash of pepper
1 teaspoon grated onion
Pinch of savory
3 to 4 teaspoons lemon juice
1 egg yolk, slightly beaten

* About 1½ cups when cooked and drained.

Cook peas and shrimp separately as directed on packages. Drain. Melt butter in saucepan. Add flour and blend until smooth. Gradually add milk; cook and stir over medium heat until thickened. Add salt, pepper, onion, savory, and lemon juice. Stir to blend. Pour small amount of hot mixture over egg yolk; blend. Return to saucepan and cook 1 minute. Add peas and shrimp to sauce and cook just to heat through. Serve on toast points. Garnish with parsley, if desired. Makes 5 servings.
PREPARE-AHEAD HINT. Make white sauce and heat through at meal-preparation time. Cook peas and shrimp, add to hot sauce, and proceed as directed.

Baked Fish with Tomato Sauce

Serve with succotash, cucumbers in sour cream, French bread, and Strawberry-Rhubarb Cobbler (p. 60).

2 packages (12 ounces each) Birds Eye
  Flounder, Haddock, or Cod Fillets,
  partly thawed
2 tablespoons minced onion
1 garlic clove, minced
1 tablespoon butter
2 cans (8 ounces each) tomato sauce
1 teaspoon sugar
½ teaspoon Worcestershire sauce
2 tablespoons lemon juice
Chopped parsley

Cut fish into 6 portions. Arrange in greased shallow baking dish. Sauté onion and garlic in butter until tender and transparent. Add tomato sauce, sugar, Worcestershire sauce, and lemon juice. Simmer 5 minutes. Pour over fish. Bake in hot oven (400°F.) 20 to 25 minutes. Sprinkle with chopped parsley, if desired. Makes 6 servings.
PREPARE-AHEAD HINT. Make sauce and simmer as directed. Spoon over fish before baking.

Any vegetable-shy members in your family? Treat them to Green Beans Amandine (p. 31) and be ready to serve seconds.

SECTION 3

GENERAL FOODS
KITCHENS

Vegetables

Compare old cookbooks with new and you're surprised at the number of vegetable recipes our modern versions contain. It's not just that we today are more aware of nutrition — (and vegetables *are* good for us). We've discovered that vegetables rightly cooked and nicely seasoned have their own special summer flavor needed to round out any meal, whatever the occasion or time of year.

More and more, vegetable plates are appearing as entrées on restaurant menus. And there's no reason why you can't serve vegetable plates at home. Four or five different vegetables make a colorful service and offer contrast in textures. Be sure to anticipate your top-of-the-stove and oven space needed for preparation. You will find directions here for cooking vegetables in the oven and also by an excellent method known as the butter-boil.

One thing more in praise of vegetables: they offer many ways to be creative in cookery. Here, along with some of General Foods Kitchens' favorite recipes, are suggestions for experimenting on your own.

The Creative Touch. There are many ways to be creative in vegetable cookery — or any other kind for that matter. You may . . .

Change the flavor with spices or herbs, lemon or orange juice, bacon-vinegar-and-oil, or any favorite French dressing.

Add a flavor contrast with sauces such as cheese sauce or white sauces of various kinds or butter flavored with lemon, orange, or garlic.

Add a texture contrast by combining the cooked vegetable with toasted almonds, chopped pecans, water chestnuts, celery, onion, green pepper, pimiento, sautéed mushrooms, crisp bacon, or ham bits.

Change the shape by serving in a casserole mixture, by making into timbales or mounds, by slicing or cutting a new way, by French-frying.

Add a different garnish such as capers, seived hard-cooked eggs, crisp well-buttered croutons, grated or shaved cheese.

Change the role in the meal by serving the vegetable as a garnish for meats. Or use in a salad or a soup, a soufflé, or stew. At least one vegetable — squash — may be made into dessert.

Before you begin to experiment, read many recipes and look over the seasonings suggestions on p. 96 to familiarize yourself with the flavors suited to each other. Try new ideas on a small amount of vegetable first.

Green Beans Amandine

Italian green beans mixed with butter-toasted almonds.

1 package (9 ounces) Birds Eye Italian
  Green Beans
¼ cup slivered blanched almonds
2 tablespoons butter

Cook beans as directed on package; drain. Meanwhile, sauté almonds in butter until golden brown. Add to beans and mix lightly. Makes 3 servings.

Italian Green Beans and Water Chestnuts

How and where do you buy water chestnuts? In cans at your supermarket.

½ cup (5-ounce can) water chestnuts,
  drained and sliced
2 tablespoons butter
1 package (9 ounces) Birds Eye Italian
  Green Beans
¼ cup water
½ beef bouillon cube

Sauté chestnuts in butter in a saucepan for 2 to 3 minutes. Add beans, mixing well. Add water and bouillon cube. Bring to a boil and simmer 5 minutes. Makes 3 servings.

Savory Wax Beans and Rice

A quick-and-easy meal brightener for busy days.

1 package (9 ounces) Birds Eye Cut
  Wax Beans
2 cups (1-pound can) stewed tomatoes
  (with peppers, onions, and seasonings)
⅓ cup Minute Rice*
1 tablespoon butter

* Measure right from box.

Cook wax beans according to package directions. Drain. Combine beans, stewed tomatoes, Minute Rice, and

butter in saucepan and bring to boil over medium heat. Reduce heat and simmer, stirring occasionally, about 10 minutes, or until rice is tender. Makes 4 to 6 servings.

Vegetable Casserole Royale

A delightful mixture of rice, broccoli or asparagus, almonds, and tomato with an unusual topping.

1⅓ cups Minute Rice
½ teaspoon salt
1⅓ cups boiling water
1 package (10 ounces) Birds Eye
  Chopped Broccoli*
3 tablespoons slivered or chopped
  blanched almonds
3 tablespoons butter
2 tomatoes, sliced
Salt, pepper, melted butter
1 egg white
¾ cup mayonnaise

* Or use 1 package (10 ounces) Birds Eye Asparagus Cuts. Cook, drain, and chop.

Add Minute Rice and salt to boiling water in saucepan. Mix just to moisten all rice. Cover and remove from heat. Let stand 5 minutes.

Meanwhile, cook vegetable. Drain. Sauté almonds in butter until golden brown. Add to rice, mixing lightly with a fork. Add broccoli or chopped asparagus and mix well. Spoon into greased 1½-quart casserole. Arrange sliced tomatoes over top. Season tomatoes with salt and pepper and brush with melted butter. Place casserole under broiler 8 to 10 minutes, or until tomatoes are lightly browned.

Meanwhile, beat egg white until it will stand in soft peaks. Add mayonnaise and blend well. Spread over tomatoes and return casserole to broiler for 2 minutes, or until topping is golden brown. Makes 5 or 6 servings.

PREPARE-AHEAD HINT. Blanch almonds and sliver or chop and wrap in foil.

Broccoli Italienne

Very tasty with roast lamb or chops, baked chicken breasts, or pot roast.

1 package (10 ounces) Birds Eye
   Chopped Broccoli or Broccoli Spears
2 tablespoons olive oil or melted butter
1 tablespoon lemon juice
1 small clove garlic, minced

Cook broccoli as directed on the package. Drain well. Combine olive oil, lemon juice, and garlic and pour over the broccoli. Mix lightly. Serve at once. Makes 3 servings.

Spinach-Stuffed Tomatoes

Excellent with broiled or baked fish or sea-food casserole.

1 package (10 ounces) Birds Eye
   Chopped Spinach
6 to 8 firm ripe tomatoes
3 tablespoons butter or margarine
3 tablespoons flour
1 teaspoon salt
½ teaspoon dry mustard
¼ teaspoon Worcestershire sauce
Dash of pepper
2 hard-cooked eggs, diced
Buttered soft bread crumbs

Cook spinach as directed on the package and drain. Remove pulp from stem end of tomatoes and set aside. Sprinkle inside of tomatoes with salt. Invert and let stand about 10 minutes to drain.

   Meanwhile, melt butter or margarine in saucepan. Add flour and seasonings; mix well. Then add cooked spinach, eggs, and tomato pulp; mix well. Fill tomato shells with spinach mixture. Top with buttered crumbs. Place in a buttered shallow baking dish and bake in a hot oven (400°F.) about 15 minutes, or until tomatoes are tender and topping is browned. Or, if desired, bake in moderate oven (350°F.) for 20 to 25

minutes, or until done. Serves 6 to 8.
Note: For flavor variation, add a pinch of oregano to each tomato shell before filling with the spinach mixture.

Broccoli-Stuffed Tomatoes. Use above recipe but substitute 1 package (10 ounces) Birds Eye Chopped Broccoli for the spinach.

Asparagus-Stuffed Tomatoes. Use above recipe but substitute 1 package (10 ounces) Birds Eye Asparagus Cuts for the spinach.

PREPARE-AHEAD HINT. Stuff tomatoes and refrigerate. At meal-preparation time, top tomatoes with buttered soft bread crumbs and bake as directed.

Spinach Casserole

Spinach-in-casserole, baked in a white sauce with hard-cooked eggs and a cheese-crumb topping.

1 package (10 ounces) Birds Eye
   Chopped Spinach
1 tablespoon chopped onion
1 clove garlic, minced
½ cup chopped mushrooms
2 tablespoons butter or other fat
2 tablespoons flour
1 cup milk
2 hard-cooked eggs, chopped
½ teaspoon salt
Dash of pepper
½ cup buttered bread crumbs
1 tablespoon grated Parmesan cheese

Cook spinach as directed on the package. Drain. Sauté onion, garlic, and mushrooms in butter until tender. Stir in flour. Gradually add milk, blending well, and cook until mixture is thickened, stirring constantly. Add spinach, eggs, salt, and pepper. Pour into a greased casserole. Combine bread crumbs and cheese. Sprinkle over spinach. Place under broiler until crumbs are browned — about 5 minutes. Makes 3 or 4 servings.

PREPARE-AHEAD HINT. Make sauce

Tender, frozen peas and a little ingenuity produce delightful dishes. For others, see The Creative Touch, p. 30.

with onion, garlic, and mushrooms as directed and refrigerate. Hard-cook eggs. At meal-preparation time, reheat sauce, cook spinach, drain, and add with the chopped hard-cooked eggs and seasonings to the sauce. Proceed as directed in recipe.

Spinach Ring

A spinach mixture, baked in a ring mold and then unmolded. May be served plain or with a sauce.

2 packages (10 ounces each) Birds Eye
  Leaf or Chopped Spinach
Dash of pepper
1½ teaspoons minced onion
¼ cup butter, melted
2 eggs, slightly beaten

Cook spinach as directed on the package. Drain. Add pepper, onion, butter, and egg and mix very thoroughly. Spoon

into a well-greased small ring mold. Place in pan of hot water and bake in moderate oven (375°F.) 30 minutes, or until firm. Unmold. Serve plain or with a vegetable sauce. (Or fill center with scrambled eggs and bacon; serve as a main dish.) Makes 4 servings.

PREPARE-AHEAD HINT. If desired, prepare mixture and refrigerate. Then bake as directed at meal-preparation time.

Asparagus and Almond Sauce

Toasted almonds and asparagus in a cream sauce, served on rice. Especially good with turkey or chicken.

1 package (10 ounces) Birds Eye
  Asparagus Cuts or Spears*
¼ cup butter
¼ cup slivered blanched almonds
3 tablespoons flour
1 cup milk
1 cup light cream or top milk
¾ teaspoon salt
Dash of pepper
2 cups Minute Rice
2 cups water
¾ teaspoon salt
2 tablespoons butter

* Or use Birds Eye Cut Green Beans, French Style Green Beans, or Green Peas.

Cook asparagus as directed on package. Drain. Meanwhile, melt ¼ cup butter in saucepan. Add almonds and sauté until golden brown, stirring constantly. Remove almonds and set aside. Add flour to butter remaining in saucepan; blend well. Then add milk gradually, stirring constantly. Add cream, salt, and pepper. Cook and stir over low heat until sauce is smooth and thickened. Add asparagus and almonds. Prepare Minute Rice with water and salt as directed on package. Add 2 tablespoons butter and toss lightly. Serve asparagus-almond sauce on buttered rice. Makes about 3½ cups sauce, or 6 servings.

PREPARE-AHEAD HINT. Make almond sauce. Reheat at serving time and add the cooked asparagus.

Dixie Peas

A mixed vegetable dish with just a nip of Worcestershire sauce.

¼ cup butter
⅓ cup chopped onion
1½ cups thinly sliced celery
1 package (1 pound) Birds Eye
  Green Peas*
2 tablespoons hot water
¾ teaspoon salt
Dash of pepper
Dash of thyme
½ teaspoon Worcestershire sauce
2 tablespoons diced pimiento (optional)
1 tablespoon chopped parsley

* Or use 1 package (10 ounces) Birds Eye Green
Peas and reduce butter to 3 tablespoons.

Melt butter in saucepan; add onion and
celery, and sauté slowly about 5 minutes, or until onion is golden brown.
Add peas, water, salt, pepper, and
thyme. Cover and simmer 6 to 8 minutes, or until peas are just tender; (do
not overcook). Add Worcestershire
sauce, pimiento, and parsley, mixing
lightly. Makes 6 to 8 servings.
PREPARE-AHEAD HINT. Chop onion and
slice celery. Wrap in foil and refrigerate until ready to cook. If desired,
dice pimiento and chop the parsley
ahead of time, too.

Peas Savory

*Peas, seasoned with herb, and baked
with mushrooms and onion.*

1 package (1 pound) Birds Eye
  Green Peas*
⅔ cup (4-ounce can) sliced
  mushrooms, drained
1 tablespoon finely chopped onion
¾ teaspoon salt
Dash of pepper
¼ teaspoon savory
2 tablespoons butter

* Or use 10-ounce package and decrease salt to
½ teaspoon. Bake about 35 minutes.

34

Place frozen peas in a baking dish. Add
remaining ingredients. Cover and bake
in moderate oven (375°F.) until just
tender — about 1 hour. Stir before
serving. Makes 5 or 6 servings.

Vegetables Supreme

*Sautéed almonds, mushrooms, and
chopped onion mixed with peas, green
beans, or wax beans.*

1 package (10 ounces or 1 pound)
  Birds Eye Green Peas*
¼ cup slivered blanched almonds
1½ cups sliced fresh mushrooms
¼ cup chopped onion
3 tablespoons butter
¼ teaspoon salt

* Or use Birds Eye Whole Green Beans, French
Style Green Beans, Cut Green Beans, Cut Wax
Beans, or Italian Green Beans.

Cook peas as directed on package;
drain. Sauté almonds, mushrooms, and
onion in butter until the mushrooms
are tender. Combine peas, almond-
onion-mushroom mixture, and salt. Mix
lightly. Makes 3 or 4 servings with
small package and 6 to 8 servings with
large package.
PREPARE-AHEAD HINT. Blanch and
sliver almonds. Slice mushrooms and
chop onion. Wrap in separate foil
packets; refrigerate until ready to use.

Squash Baked with Marshmallows

A favorite recipe with teen-agers.

1 package (12 ounces) Birds Eye
  Cooked Squash, thawed
2 tablespoons melted butter
¾ teaspoon salt
Dash of pepper
⅛ teaspoon cinnamon
Dash of nutmeg
1 egg yolk, slightly beaten
6 marshmallows

Combine squash, butter, seasonings, and egg yolk. Spoon into buttered shallow baking dish. Arrange marshmallows on top. Place in pan of hot water and bake in moderate oven (375°F.) 20 minutes, or until marshmallows are browned and partially melted. Makes 3 servings.

PREPARE-AHEAD HINT. Make squash mixture and refrigerate. At meal-preparation time, spoon into casserole, top with marshmallows, and bake.

Horse-Radish Limas in Cream

Perfect with beef, ham, or tongue.

1 package (10 ounces)
  Birds Eye Baby Lima Beans
2 tablespoons chopped onion
2 tablespoons butter, melted
½ to ⅔ cup light cream
2 sprigs parsley, chopped
Dash of nutmeg
Dash of pepper
¼ teaspoon salt
2 to 3 teaspoons horse-radish

Cook Lima beans as directed on package. Drain.

Meanwhile, sauté onion in butter until tender, but not brown. Add remaining ingredients and heat thoroughly. Pour over cooked Limas and serve. Makes 3 or 4 servings.

Squash and Onion Savory

A company dish of nicely seasoned winter squash, garnished with French fried onion rings, to serve 12.

3 packages (12 ounces each)
  Birds Eye Cooked Squash
3 tablespoons chopped onion
6 tablespoons butter or margarine
1½ teaspoons salt
⅛ teaspoon pepper
3 packages (4 ounces each)
  Birds Eye French Fried Onion Rings

Place squash in top of double boiler. Sauté chopped onion in 3 tablespoons butter until lightly browned and tender. Add to the squash with remaining butter and the salt and pepper. Cover and heat over boiling water until completely thawed and hot throughout, about 35 minutes. Stir often. Spread onion rings on baking sheet. Bake in a moderate oven (375°F.) for 10 minutes. Turn onions carefully and bake 5 minutes longer. Serve squash with onion rings as garnish. Makes 12 servings.

Asparagus-Stuffed Eggplant

Eggplant mixed with asparagus cuts, seasonings, bread cubes, ham, and cheese and baked in the eggplant shells.

1 package (10 ounces) Birds Eye
  Asparagus Cuts
1 medium eggplant, split lengthwise
2 tablespoons chopped onion
1 small clove garlic, minced
1 cup chopped celery
2 tablespoons butter
1 cup diced cooked ham
1¼ cups small bread cubes
¼ cup grated cheese
⅛ teaspoon pepper
Salt

Cook asparagus as directed on package. Drain. Scoop inside from eggplant and cut in 1-inch pieces, reserving shells. Cook eggplant pieces in boiling water until tender. Drain. Sauté onion, garlic, and celery in butter until tender and transparent. Add to eggplant; then add asparagus, ham, 1 cup of the bread cubes, the cheese, pepper, and salt to taste. Fill eggplant shells lightly and top with remaining bread cubes. Bake in moderate oven (375°F.) for 30 minutes, or until golden brown. Serves 4.

PREPARE-AHEAD HINT. Cook vegetables and mix with remaining ingredients as directed. Stuff eggplant shells. Bake at meal-preparation time.

Frozen vegetables cook beautifully in oven along with roasts, soufflés, and casseroles. For directions, see p. 42.

see p. 42.

Creole Lima Beans

Good with veal chops, sautéed shrimp and rice, or baked or broiled fish.

1 package (10 ounces or 1 pound)
  Birds Eye Fordhook or
  Baby Lima Beans
⅓ cup diced onion
⅓ cup diced green pepper
⅓ cup butter
1½ cups canned tomatoes
¾ teaspoon salt
Dash of pepper
¼ teaspoon sugar

Cook Lima beans as directed on package; drain. Meanwhile, sauté onion and green pepper in butter until tender. Add Lima beans, tomatoes, seasonings, and sugar. Simmer 3 to 5 minutes. Makes 4 to 6 servings with 10-ounce package; 6 to 8 servings with 1-pound package.

Lyonnaise Vegetable Casserole

For supper or luncheon, serve with strips of crisp bacon, warm French bread, and a jellied salad.

1 package (10 ounces) Birds Eye
  Mixed Garden Vegetables
1 package (10 ounces) Birds Eye
  Cauliflower
½ cup onion rings
5 tablespoons butter
3 tablespoons flour
½ teaspoon salt
Dash of pepper
1 cup milk
1 cup (4 ounces) grated
  American cheese
1 tablespoon chopped pimiento
½ cup bread cubes

Cook mixed vegetables and cauliflower as directed on packages; drain. Mean-

36

while, sauté onion rings in 3 table-spoons of the butter until lightly browned. Blend in flour, salt, and pepper. Add milk gradually and bring to a boil over low heat, stirring constantly. Add cheese and pimiento; stir until smooth. Remove from heat. Arrange mixed vegetables and cauliflower in a 1½-quart greased shallow casserole. Melt remaining 2 tablespoons butter, add bread cubes, and toast lightly. Pour cheese sauce over vegetables and top with toasted bread cubes. Bake in moderate oven (375°F.) for 15 minutes, or until bubbly. Makes 6 to 8 servings.
PREPARE-AHEAD HINT. Cook vegetables. Make cheese sauce with onion and pimiento as directed. Toast bread cubes. At meal-preparation time, arrange vegetables in casserole, add cheese sauce, top with toasted bread cubes, and bake as directed, adding about 10 minutes to baking time.

Cauliflower and Tomatoes

Cauliflower cooked with tomatoes, olive oil, and garlic and sprinkled with grated Parmesan cheese.

1 package (10 ounces)
  Birds Eye Cauliflower
1½ cups boiling water, salted
1 small clove garlic
3 tablespoons olive oil
½ teaspoon salt
½ cup canned tomatoes
1 teaspoon chopped parsley
2 tablespoons grated Parmesan cheese

Place frozen cauliflower in boiling salted water just long enough to separate florets (about 3 to 4 minutes). Drain. Sauté garlic in olive oil until browned. Remove garlic; add florets to olive oil and sauté lightly. Add salt and tomatoes, cover, and simmer 2 minutes. Arrange in serving dish; sprinkle with parsley and grated cheese. Serves 3.

Spring Corn

Try with sliced baked ham or sliced tongue and a mixed green salad.

1 package (10 ounces or 1 pound)
  Birds Eye Whole Kernel Corn
¼ cup chopped onion
2 tablespoons butter
Dash of pepper
½ teaspoon sugar
⅛ or ¼ teaspoon dry mustard
½ or ¾ teaspoon salt
1 or 2 tablespoons chopped parsley

Cook corn as directed on the package; drain. Sauté the onion in butter until golden brown. Stir in pepper, sugar, mustard, and salt. Add corn and parsley and mix well. Makes 3 or 4 servings with 10-ounce package; 5 or 6 servings with 1-pound package.
PREPARE-AHEAD HINT. Chop onion and parsley, wrap in foil, and refrigerate until ready to use.

Corn Pudding

For supper dish, make pudding with Cheddar cheese and serve with well-browned link sausages.

1 package (10 ounces) Birds Eye
  Whole Kernel Corn
3 eggs
2 tablespoons flour
1 tablespoon sugar
2 tablespoons butter, melted
1½ cups milk
1 teaspoon salt
⅛ teaspoon pepper
1 cup grated Cheddar cheese (optional)

Cook corn as directed on package. Drain. Beat eggs slightly, add cooked corn and the flour, and blend well. Mix in remaining ingredients. Pour into greased 1-quart baking dish. Set in a pan of hot water and bake in moderate oven (350°F.) about 1 hour and 20 minutes, or until firm. Serves 6.

Creamed Peas and Mushrooms

Peas and mushrooms in white sauce, seasoned with grated onion and a hint of nutmeg.

1 package (10 ounces or 1 pound)
    Birds Eye Green Peas
¼ pound fresh mushrooms, sliced
¼ teaspoon grated onion
3 tablespoons butter
2 tablespoons flour
1 cup light cream or milk
½ teaspoon salt
Dash of pepper
Dash of nutmeg

Cook peas as directed on package; drain. Sauté mushrooms and onion in butter until mushrooms are tender. Add flour and stir until blended; then add cream or milk gradually and cook and stir over medium heat until thickened. Add salt, pepper, nutmeg, and the peas; heat thoroughly. Makes 3 or 4 servings with 10-ounce package; 5 or 6 servings with 1-pound package.

PREPARE-AHEAD HINT. Make sauce with mushrooms as directed. Refrigerate. Just before serving, cook peas, add salt, pepper, nutmeg, and peas to sauce, and heat as directed.

Tomato Vegetable Casserole

An interesting combination of Lima beans or black-eye peas, tomatoes, onion, and salt pork.

1 package (10 ounces) Birds Eye
    Fordhook Lima Beans or
    Birds Eye Black-Eye Peas
1½ tablespoons finely diced salt pork
¼ cup coarsely chopped onion
½ teaspoon salt
⅛ teaspoon pepper
¼ teaspon dry mustard
½ teaspoon sugar
1 can (1 pound) tomatoes

Cook Lima beans or black-eye peas as directed on package. Cook until very tender, adding a small amount of boiling water, if necessary. Drain. Fry salt pork until crisp. Remove from pan and set aside. Add onion to pan drippings and cook until transparent. Combine beans or peas, salt pork, onion, seasonings, sugar, and tomatoes in 1-quart casserole. Cover and bake in moderate oven (375°F.) for 1 hour. Then remove cover and bake 15 minutes longer. Serve with frankfurters, if desired. Makes 4 to 6 servings.

PREPARE-AHEAD HINT. Prepare vegetable mixture and bake, covered, for 1 hour. Cool and refrigerate. At meal-preparation time, bake, uncovered, until thoroughly heated.

Vegetables au Gratin

A colorful casserole of mixed vegetables in a cheese sauce, topped with crisp buttered crumbs.

1 package (10 ounces) Birds Eye
    Peas and Carrots
1 package (10 ounces) Birds Eye
    Whole Kernel Corn
Milk
2 tablespoons chopped onion
¼ cup butter
5 tablespoons flour
1 teaspoon salt
Dash of pepper
1 cup grated sharp American cheese
1 cup buttered bread crumbs
Paprika

Cook the peas and carrots and the corn as directed on the packages. Drain and add milk to liquid to make 2 cups. Brown onion slightly in butter. Blend in flour, stirring until smooth. Gradually blend in the milk mixture and cook until thickened, stirring constantly. Remove from heat. Add salt, pepper, and cheese and stir until cheese is melted.

Add vegetables and turn into a buttered 1½-quart casserole. Top with buttered crumbs and sprinkle with paprika. Brown under broiler. Or place casserole in pan of hot water and bake in hot oven (450°F.) 20 minutes, or until browned. Makes 6 to 8 servings. **PREPARE-AHEAD HINT.** Make casserole but do not bake. At meal-preparation time, top with the buttered crumbs and bake, allowing about 10 minutes more than called for in recipe.

age. Place in small mounds on top of a hot casserole mixture — meat, fish, or poultry. Or flute around rim of hot casserole. Bake, uncovered, in moderate oven (350°F.) for 10 minutes, or until potatoes are lightly browned. Makes 3 servings of potatoes.
Note: If desired, top each mound with a small cube of Cheddar cheese or a sprinkling of chopped chives or parsley before heating in oven.

Corn and Peas in Cream

Excellent with meat loaf and hashed brown potatoes.

1 tablespoon diced onion
1 tablespoon butter
1½ teaspoons salt
⅛ teaspoon pepper
1 package (10 ounces) Birds Eye
   Whole Kernel Corn
1 package (1 pound)
   Birds Eye Green Peas
1 cup light cream
1 cup ham, cut in thin strips
1 tablespoon butter

Sauté onion in butter until tender (about 5 minutes). Add seasonings and corn and cook, stirring occasionally with fork to separate corn. Cook 3 to 5 minutes, or until corn is tender.

Cook peas as directed on package; drain. Combine with corn; add cream gradually and heat a few minutes longer.

Sauté ham in butter and sprinkle over peas and corn. Serves 6 to 8.

Potato Topping

Whipped potatoes, mounded on any favorite hot casserole dish and browned lightly in oven.

Heat 1 package (12 ounces) Birds Eye Whipped Potatoes as directed on pack-

Corn and Green Beans in Cheese Sauce

No easier way to dress up vegetables for company or holiday meals than with a piquant cheese sauce.

1 package (10 ounces or 1 pound)
   Birds Eye Whole Kernel Corn
1 package (9 ounces) Birds Eye
   Cut Green Beans
3 tablespoons butter
3 tablespoons flour
¼ teaspoon paprika
1 or 1½ teaspoons salt
Dash of pepper
¼ teaspoon Worcestershire sauce
1½ cups milk
½ cup grated sharp Cheddar cheese

Cook the corn and the green beans as directed on the packages. Drain. Melt the butter in a saucepan. Add the flour and seasonings and stir until blended. Add milk gradually, blending well. Cook and stir over medium heat until smooth and thickened. Add cheese and stir until cheese is melted. Add vegetables and heat thoroughly. Makes 6 to 8 servings with 10-ounce package and 8 to 10 servings with 1-pound package. **PREPARE-AHEAD HINT.** Make cheese sauce and refrigerate. At meal-preparation time, cook vegetables; reheat sauce in double boiler; then heat thoroughly with vegetables as directed.

Okra Pilaf

Rice, okra, onions, green pepper, and tomatoes, flavored with bacon.

1 package (10 ounces) Birds Eye
  Whole Baby Okra
4 slices bacon, diced
½ cup chopped onions
⅓ cup chopped green pepper
2¼ cups (1 pound 4 ounces)
  canned tomatoes
1⅓ cups Minute Rice
1 teaspoon salt
Dash of pepper
2 chicken bouillon cubes, dissolved in
  1⅓ cups boiling water

Thaw okra enough to separate pods. Cut in ½-inch pieces. Fry bacon in skillet until browned. Add okra, onions, and green pepper and sauté about 5 minutes. Then add tomatoes, Minute Rice, salt, pepper, and bouillon, mixing well with a fork. Bring quickly to a boil over high heat. Then cover and simmer 5 minutes. Makes 4 servings. PREPARE-AHEAD HINT. Mix all ingredients except rice. Just before serving time, add rice, heat to boiling and simmer 5 minutes.

Potato Pancakes

Potato pancakes often take the place of potatoes or rice in a meal. But you may serve them, too, with applesauce and sausage links as a supper dish.

1 package (12 ounces) Birds Eye
  Potato Patties, thawed
2 eggs, slightly beaten
¼ cup milk
2 tablespoons flour
½ teaspoon salt
Dash of pepper

Combine ingredients in bowl, stirring just until mixed. Drop by tablespoon-fuls onto hot shallow fat in a skillet or on griddle. Cook until browned on both sides, turning once. Makes 18 to 20 small pancakes.

Marinated Vegetables

Good with fish, baked potatoes, celery and olives, and a fruit dessert.

1 package (9 ounces) Birds Eye
  Whole Green Beans*
1 package (9 ounces) Birds Eye
  Artichoke Hearts (optional)
2 medium cooked carrots
½ cup vinegar
½ cup water
¼ cup olive oil
1½ teaspoons salt
Dash of pepper
1 teaspoon sugar
½ teaspoon Worcestershire sauce
½ medium Bermuda onion, sliced

* Or use 1 package (9 ounces) Birds Eye French Style Green Beans.

Cook green beans and artichokes as directed on packages. Drain. Cook carrots and slice diagonally. (Or use left-over cooked carrots.) Combine vinegar, water, olive oil, salt, pepper, sugar, Worcestershire sauce, and onion in a saucepan and bring mixture just to a boil. Place cooked vegetables in a 1½-quart casserole. Cover with marinade and chill at least 3 hours to blend flavors. Makes 6 servings. PREPARE-AHEAD HINT. Entire recipe may be made ahead.

Creamy Hashed Brown Potatoes

An easy hot-dish for lunches, Sunday brunch, or summer days.

1 package (12 ounces) Birds Eye
  Potato Patties
3 tablespoons butter or margarine
⅓ cup light cream
Dash of pepper

Fry frozen potato patties in butter over medium heat about 5 minutes, breaking up the patties with fork or turner as the potatoes brown. Add cream and pepper and mix well. Continue to cook until potatoes are tender and brown — about 10 minutes longer. Serves 2.

Potatoes and Cheese

Cubes of cheese melted in whipped potatoes and mixed with parsley.

1 package (12 ounces) Birds Eye
  Whipped Potatoes
¼ cup cubed mild or sharp
  Cheddar cheese
1 tablespoon chopped parsley

Heat whipped potatoes in double boiler or in oven as directed on the package. Fold in cheese and parsley and return to heat for about 5 minutes, or until cheese is partly melted. Stir and serve. Makes 2 or 3 servings.

Butter-Boil Directions for Vegetables

Vegetables with a good buttery flavor, cooked a new way to preserve their bright fresh color and conserve vitamins and minerals.

Use 1 package of any of the Birds Eye vegetables listed (p. 42). In medium saucepan with tight-fitting cover, place about 2 tablespoons water (to about ⅛-inch depth). Add 1 tablespoon butter or margarine, ½ teaspoon salt, and the frozen vegetable. Cover tightly.

Bring quickly to a boil over high heat. (If necessary, separate block with fork to hasten thawing.) Then reduce heat to low and simmer until vegetable is just tender. Use cooking time given (p. 42) as guide. Stir occasionally to prevent sticking. If necessary, add a small amount of water during cooking. Do not overcook. Serve at once. Makes about 3 servings.

Nicely cooked and served, vegetables appeal to everyone. For the sauce served on asparagus, see Fluffy Orange Butter (p. 81).

Vegetable	Cooking Time
Corn, Whole Kernel—(10 oz.)	About 2 min.
Green Beans, Cut—(9 or 10 oz.)	10 to 12 min.
Green Beans, French Style—	
(9 or 10 oz.)	8 to 10 min.
Green Peas—(10 oz.)*	5 to 7 min.
Lima Beans, Fordhook—	
(10 oz.)**	10 to 12 min.
Mixed Garden Vegetables—	
(10 oz.)	8 to 10 min.
Peas and Carrots—(10 oz.)	6 to 8 min.
Wax Beans, Cut—(9 oz.)	8 to 10 min.

*Use 1 tablespoon water
**Use ¼ cup water

Oven Directions for Vegetables

Bake with other oven dishes at 325°F., 350°F., or 375°F. (see directions below).

For each package (9, 10, or 12 oz.) Birds Eye vegetables, use 1 to 2 tablespoons butter or margarine and ¼ teaspoon salt. (Blocks of spinach and chopped broccoli should be cut into 6 or 8 pieces.)

Place ingredients in a baking dish. Cover and bake in moderate oven (350°F.) until just tender. See chart for approximate baking time. Increase time about 10 minutes for oven at 325°F. and decrease about 10 minutes for oven at 375°F. Makes about 3 delicious servings.

Vegetable	Cooking Time at 350°F.
Asparagus Cuts—(10 oz.)	55 to 60 min.
Asparagus Spears—(10 oz.)	55 to 60 min.
Broccoli, Chopped—(10 oz.)	45 to 50 min.
Broccoli Spears—(10 oz.)	40 to 45 min.
Brussels Sprouts—(10 oz.)	40 to 45 min.
Cauliflower—(10 oz.)	50 to 55 min.
Corn, Whole Kernel—(10 oz.)	45 to 50 min.
Green Beans, Cut—(9 oz.)	55 to 60 min.
Green Beans, French Style—(9 oz.)	55 to 60 min.
Green Peas—(10 oz.)	45 to 50 min.
Lima Beans, Baby—(10 oz.)*	55 to 60 min.
Lima Beans, Fordhook—(10 oz.)**	45 to 50 min.
Mixed Garden Vegetables—(10 oz.)	60 min.

*Add ¼ cup water with butter and salt.
**Add 2 tablespoons water with butter and salt.

Vegetable	Cooking Time at 350°F.
Peas and Carrots—(10 oz.)	55 to 60 min.
Spinach, Chopped or Leaf—(10 oz.)	45 to 50 min.
Squash, Cooked—(12 oz.)	45 min.
Succotash—(10 oz.)	55 to 60 min.
Wax Beans, Cut—(9 oz.)	60 min.

High-Altitude Cookery Butter-Boil Directions for Vegetables

Cut Green Beans. Use 1 package (9 ounces) Birds Eye Cut Green Beans. In medium saucepan with tight-fitting cover, place frozen vegetable, 2 to 4 tablespoons water, ½ teaspoon salt, and 1 tablespoon butter or margarine. Cover tightly and cook over low heat until water begins to simmer. (If necessary, separate block with fork to hasten thawing.)

Simmer very gently for 18 to 20 minutes, or until vegetable is tender. Stir occasionally to prevent sticking. If necessary, add a small amount of water during cooking. Makes about 3 servings.

French Style Green Beans. Use 1 package (9 ounces) Birds Eye French Style Green Beans. In medium saucepan with tight-fitting cover, place frozen vegetable, 2 to 4 tablespoons water, ½ teaspoon salt, and 1 tablespoon butter or margarine. Cover tightly and cook over low heat until water begins to simmer. (If necessary, separate block with fork to hasten thawing.)

Simmer very gently for 14 to 16 minutes, or until vegetable is tender. Stir occasionally to prevent sticking. If necessary, add a small amount of water during cooking. Makes about 3 servings.

Whole Kernel Corn. Use 1 package (10 ounces) Birds Eye Whole Kernel Corn. In medium saucepan with tight-fitting cover, place frozen vegetable, 2 to 4 tablespoons water, ½ teaspoon salt, and 1 tablespoon butter or margarine. Cover tightly and cook over low heat until water begins to simmer. (If necessary, separate block with fork to hasten thawing.)

Simmer very gently for 5 to 8 minutes, or until vegetable is tender. Stir occasionally to prevent sticking. If necessary, add a small amount of water during cooking. Makes about 3 servings.

Fordhook Lima Beans. Use 1 package (10 ounces) Birds Eye Fordhook Lima Beans. In medium saucepan with tight-fitting cover, place frozen vegetable, 4 to 6 tablespoons water, ½ teaspoon salt, and 1 tablespoon butter or margarine. Cover tightly and cook over low heat until water begins to simmer. (If necessary, separate block with fork to hasten thawing.)

Simmer very gently 18 to 20 minutes, or until vegetable is tender. Stir occasionally to prevent sticking. If necessary, add a small amount of water during cooking. Makes about 3 servings.

Mixed Garden Vegetables. Use 1 package (10 ounces) Birds Eye Mixed Garden Vegetables. In medium saucepan with tight-fitting cover, place frozen vegetables, 4 to 6 tablespoons water, ½ teaspoon salt, and 1 tablespoon butter or margarine. Cover tightly and cook over low heat until water begins to simmer. (If necessary, separate block with fork to hasten thawing.)

Simmer very gently 18 to 20 minutes, or until vegetables are tender. Stir occasionally to prevent sticking. If necessary, add a small amount of water during cooking. Makes about 3 servings.

Green Peas. Use 1 package (10 ounces) Birds Eye Green Peas. In medium saucepan with tight-fitting cover, place frozen vegetable, 1 to 2 tablespoons water, ½ teaspoon salt, and 1 tablespoon butter or margarine. Cover tightly and cook over low heat until water begins to simmer. (If necessary, sepa-

rate block with fork to hasten thawing.)

Simmer very gently 10 to 12 minutes, or until vegetable is tender. Stir occasionally to prevent sticking. If necessary, add a small amount of water during cooking. Makes about 3 servings.

Peas and Carrots. Use 1 package (10 ounces) Birds Eye Peas and Carrots. In medium saucepan with tight-fitting cover, place frozen vegetables, 2 to 4 tablespoons water, ½ teaspoon salt, and 1 tablespoon butter or margarine. Cover tightly and cook over low heat until water begins to simmer. (If necessary, separate block with fork to hasten thawing.)

Simmer very gently 10 to 12 minutes, or until vegetable is tender. Stir occasionally to prevent sticking. If necessary, add a small amount of water during cooking. Makes about 3 servings.

Cut Wax Beans. Use 1 package (9 ounces) Birds Eye Cut Wax Beans. In medium saucepan with tight-fitting cover, place frozen vegetable, 2 to 4 tablespoons water, ½ teaspoon salt, and 1 tablespoon butter or margarine. Cover tightly and cook over low heat until water begins to simmer. (If necessary, separate block with fork to hasten thawing.)

Simmer very gently 18 to 20 minutes, or until vegetable is tender. Stir occasionally to prevent sticking. If necessary, add a small amount of water during cooking. Makes about 3 servings.

Rule of Thumb For High Altitude Cookery

When cooking frozen vegetables at high altitudes, follow package directions but add slightly more water and increase cooking time. Use saucepan with tight-fitting cover to prevent rapid evaporation of water.

43

A good salad piques the appetite and like Artichoke Hearts in Marinade (p. 3) often serves a dual role. For buffets or smorgasbord, increase recipe and arrange in simple bowls.

SECTION 4

Salads

Salads delight the ingenious cook. There's almost no limit to the combinations you can concoct with frozen foods provided you have all fine ingredients, a good food sense, imagination, and an adventurous family.

Sometimes the salad serves as main dish, sometimes as dessert. A side salad balances the meal and provides contrast for the rest of the menu. The rule is: Hearty entrée . . . light salad. Light entrée . . . hearty salad. Always the flavor should be distinctive — savory or pleasantly tart and refreshing.

There are many ways to classify salads, but for convenience, we've indexed them as jellied, meat or poultry, sea food, and vegetable. We have indicated, too, the salads that may double as dessert.

SALAD DRESSINGS

For vegetable salads or tossed salads, use a French-type dressing, mayonnaise, or a combination of the two. The dressing blends and mellows the salad flavors.

For fruit salads, use mayonnaise, French-type dressing and mayonnaise mixed, French-type dressing made with fruit juice instead of vinegar, or mayonnaise combined with whipped cream or sour cream.

With jellied salads, serve mayonnaise or any of the mayonnaise mixtures, mentioned above.

For sea-food, poultry, or meat salads, use mayonnaise or any of the mayonnaise mixtures.

GARNISHES

Surround jellied salads with crisp greens such as lettuce, endive, or water cress. Decorate the dollop of mayonnaise with olive slice, crossed pimiento strips, a sprig of parsley or green pepper ring, or a dash of paprika.

Decorate fruit salads with a maraschino cherry, orange section, twisted orange slice, mint leaf, whole berry, or pecan half.

For sea-food, poultry, or meat salads, use tomato wedges, cucumber wedges, radish roses, green pepper rings, stuffed hard-cooked eggs, or egg slices, green onions, or celery strips.

For cooked vegetable or potato salads, use rolled thin ham slices, cocktail sausages, tiny meat balls, or celery stuffed with pimiento cheese.

Jellied Raspberry Special

Serve as dinner salad with mayonnaise, or as dessert salad with whipped cream or other dessert topping.

1 regular size package (3 ounces)
  Raspberry Jell-O Gelatin
1 cup boiling water
1 package (10 ounces) Birds Eye
  Red Raspberries
½ cup cold water
1 tablespoon lemon juice
1 medium banana, sliced

Dissolve Jell-O in boiling water. Add frozen raspberries and stir until Jell-O thickens and fruit separates. Add cold water and lemon juice. Chill until slightly thickened. Fold in bananas. Pour into individual molds. Chill until firm. Unmold. For salad, serve on crisp lettuce with mayonnaise. For dessert, serve with plain or whipped cream. Makes 6 servings.

PREPARE-AHEAD HINT. Make the night before or in the morning for serving at evening meal.

Cream Cheese and Peach Salad

For buffet suppers to serve 8, make two molds, one for each end of table.

1 package (12 ounces) Birds Eye
  Sliced Peaches, thawed
1 cup peach juice and water
1 regular size package (3 ounces)
  Orange Jell-O Gelatin
Dash of salt
1 cup boiling water
1 package (3 ounces)
  cream cheese, softened

Drain peaches. Measure juice and add cold water to make 1 cup. Dissolve

46

Jell-O and salt in boiling water. Add diluted peach juice. Add 2 tablespoons of the warm Jell-O to the softened cream cheese. Beat until thoroughly blended. Meanwhile, chill remaining Jell-O until slightly thickened.

Spoon ½ cup into a 1-quart ring mold. Arrange peach slices on top. Cover with another ½ cup Jell-O. Chill until set but not firm.

Place bowl of remaining Jell-O firmly in ice and water. Whip with sturdy beater until fluffy and thick. Beat in cream cheese mixture. Pour over Jell-O in mold. Chill until firm. Unmold and garnish with salad greens. If desired, serve with bowl of mayonnaise or salad dressing in center of mold. Serves 4.

PREPARE-AHEAD HINT. Make salad the night before serving. Gelatin unmolds best when firmly set.

Strawberry-Grapefruit Chill

So simple and so good! Serve as salad with mayonnaise or as dessert with custard sauce or other topping.

2 regular size packages (3 ounces each) Apple Jell-O Gelatin
2 cups boiling water
1 package (1 pound) Birds Eye Sliced Strawberries*
1 can (13-½ ounces) frozen grapefruit sections

* Or use 2 packages (10 ounces each) Birds Eye Strawberry Halves.

Dissolve Jell-O in boiling water. Add frozen blocks of fruit. Stir gently until fruit thaws and separates and Jell-O begins to thicken. Pour into a 9x9x2-inch pan. Chill until firm. Cut into squares; serve on crisp lettuce with mayonnaise or mayonnaise and whipped cream mixed. Makes 12 servings.

PREPARE-AHEAD HINT. Make night before or in the morning for serving at evening meal, if desired. However, with this quick-chill method, the gelatin should be firm in 1 to 1½ hours.

Jellied Vegetables in Sour Cream

Serve with veal chops or roast, asparagus spears, and strawberries and angel food cake for dessert.

1 regular size package (3 ounces) Lemon Jell-O Gelatin
2 bouillon cubes
1 cup boiling water
1 package (10 ounces) Birds Eye Peas and Carrots
1 cup sour cream
¼ cup tarragon vinegar
¼ cup green pepper strips
2 to 3 tablespoons thinly sliced scallions
½ teaspoon salt
Dash of pepper

Dissolve Jell-O and bouillon cubes in boiling water. Chill until slightly thickened. Meanwhile, cook peas and carrots as directed on package. Drain and cool. Combine with remaining ingredients and fold into slightly thickened Jell-O. Pour into a 1-quart mold or individual molds. Chill until firm. Unmold on crisp lettuce and garnish with water cress, if desired. Serve with mayonnaise. Makes 6 servings.

PREPARE-AHEAD HINT. Make early in the morning or night before.

Wax Bean Salad

Suggested menu: Cold sliced tongue, potato salad, wax bean salad, radish roses, sliced tomatoes, and hot beverage.

1 package (9 ounces) Birds Eye Cut Wax Beans
¼ cup Good Seasons Onion Salad Dressing
¼ cup coarsely diced celery
1 tablespoon chopped chives

Cook beans as directed on package. Drain. Cool. Combine beans and remaining ingredients. Chill. Serve on bed of crisp spinach, water cress, or lettuce. Makes 3 servings.

PREPARE-AHEAD HINT. Make sufficiently ahead to chill salad thoroughly.

Greek Cauliflower Salad

An arranged salad of cauliflower, tomatoes, hard-cooked egg, and endive around a center of mayonnaise.

1 package (10 ounces) Birds Eye
   Cauliflower
1 cup Good Seasons Onion
   Salad Dressing
4 medium-size tomatoes,
   peeled and quartered
⅓ cup mayonnaise
3 hard-cooked eggs, quartered
2 cups shredded green endive
Paprika

Cook cauliflower as directed on the package. Drain. Pour salad dressing over cauliflower and tomatoes in a bowl and let stand in refrigerator for about 4 hours to marinate. Place mayonnaise in center of large round platter. Arrange cauliflower around mayonnaise. Then make three encircling rings with tomatoes, hard-cooked eggs, and endive. Sprinkle paprika on the mayonnaise. Serve well chilled. Serves 6.

PREPARE-AHEAD HINT. Marinate cauliflower and tomatoes; hard-cook eggs and refrigerate in shells; wash endive.

Crab Meat Artichoke Salad

Crab meat and avocado, artichoke hearts, lettuce, and water cress with a French-type dressing.

1 package (9 ounces) Birds Eye
   Artichoke Hearts
2 cans (6½ ounces each) crab meat
2 tablespoons lemon juice
1 avocado, peeled and cut in
   bite-size pieces
3 cups (½ large head) chopped lettuce
1 cup (about 1 bunch) chopped
   water cress
Salt
Good Seasons Classic
   Salad Dressing

Chef's Summer Salad (p. 50) offers a delicious way to use up leftover ham. For an easy-do-meal, serve with hot biscuits.

Prepare artichoke hearts as directed on package. Drain, cut in halves, and chill.

Break crab meat into bite-size pieces and sprinkle with lemon juice. Then combine crab meat, avocado, lettuce, water cress, and artichoke hearts in a large salad bowl. Add salt and dressing to taste. Toss lightly. Serves 6.

PREPARE-AHEAD HINT. Cook and chill artichoke hearts. Wash greens and refrigerate. Assemble salad at meal-preparation time.

Shrimp-and-Rice Patio Salad

A very special salad of chilled rice, shrimp, avocado, and peas. Notice, too, the party-size recipe for 36.

1 package (10 ounces) Birds Eye
   Green Peas
½ teaspoon salt
1½ cups tomato juice
1⅔ cups Minute Brown Rice
   or 1⅓ cups Minute Rice
½ cup chopped dill pickle
1 teaspoon grated onion
⅛ teaspoon pepper
2 cups (about 1 pound raw) cooked
   shrimp, cut in half and chilled
1 cup sliced avocado
¾ cup mayonnaise*

* Or use ¼ cup French dressing and ½ cup mayonnaise.

Cook peas as directed on the package. Drain.

Meanwhile, combine salt and tomato juice in saucepan. Bring to a boil. Stir in Minute Rice. Cover, remove from heat, and let stand 5 minutes. Then add peas, pickle, onion, and pepper. Mix lightly with a fork. Chill.

Just before serving, add chilled shrimp, avocado, and mayonnaise. Toss together lightly. Serve on crisp salad greens. Garnish with tomato wedges, if desired. Makes 6 servings.

For party-size recipe (to serve 36), use the following:

5 packages (10 ounces each)
   Birds Eye Green Peas
2 to 3 teaspoons salt
1 can (1 quart 14 ounces) tomato juice
   plus water to make 2 quarts
7 cups (23⅛-ounce package)
   Minute Rice
2½ cups chopped dill pickles
2 tablespoons grated onion
¼ teaspoon pepper
10 cups cooked shrimp, cut in
   half — about 5 pounds fresh
5 cups avocado slices
3 cups mayonnaise
1 to 1½ cups French dressing

Make as directed in recipe at left.

PREPARE-AHEAD HINT. Prepare rice mixture with peas, pickle, onion, and pepper as directed. Chill. Cook raw shrimp and chill. Assemble salad at meal-preparation time.

Bean-Corn-and-Celery Salad

A very fine salad to serve with hamburgers or hot dogs, whether cooked indoors or out. Party-size recipe (p. 50).

1 package (10 ounces) Birds Eye
   Fordhook Lima Beans, Baby
   Lima Beans, or Butter Beans
1 package (10 ounces) Birds Eye
   Whole Kernel Corn
1 teaspoon salt
Dash of pepper
1 tablespoon vinegar
1 teaspoon grated onion
3 tablespoons sliced pimiento
2 cups sliced celery
½ cup French dressing

Cook Lima beans and corn as directed on packages. Drain and season with salt and pepper. Cool. Add vinegar, onion, pimiento, celery, and salad dressing, mixing well. Chill thoroughly. Serve on crisp lettuce. Serves 8.

For *party-size recipe* to serve 32, use 4 packages of the beans, 4 packages of the corn, 2 tablespoons minced onion, ½ cup sliced pimiento, 2 quarts diced celery, and 1 pint French dressing. Proceed as directed but omit vinegar. Season to taste.

Chef's Summer Salad. Use small recipe for Bean-Corn-and-Celery Salad, but substitute 2 packages (10 ounces each) Birds Eye Mixed Garden Vegetables for the Lima beans and corn. Arrange on serving dish with tomato slices and ham strips.

PREPARE-AHEAD HINT. Make salad hours ahead, if desired. Flavors blend as the salad chills.

Salad Vinaigrette

An arranged salad of artichoke hearts, asparagus spears, and green beans in a savory dressing.

1 package (9 ounces) Birds Eye
    Artichoke Hearts
1 package (10 ounces) Birds Eye
    Asparagus Spears
1 package (9 ounces) Birds Eye
    Cut Green Beans
Vinaigrette Dressing
1 hard-cooked egg, sliced
Pimiento strips
1 hard-cooked egg, sieved

Cook vegetables as directed on packages. Pour ¼ cup of the dressing over each. Chill about 1 hour. Arrange artichoke hearts, asparagus spears, green beans, and sliced hard-cooked egg in rows on salad plate. Add another row of pimiento strips next to green beans. Sprinkle salad with sieved hard-cooked egg. Serve with the remaining dressing. Makes 6 servings.

To make **Vinaigrette Dressing,** mix together 1 cup French dressing, 2 tablespoons chopped parsley, ¼ cup finely chopped pickle, 2 teaspoons chopped onion, and 2 teaspoons capers. Beat until blended. Chill. Makes 1½ cups.

PREPARE-AHEAD HINT. Cook vegetables. Make dressing and marinate vegetables. Cook egg and slice pimiento. Arrange salad at meal-preparation time.

Large Vegetable Salad

Cooked vegetables, raw tomatoes, and onion rings in a bleu cheese dressing. Serves 10 to 12.

1 package (10 ounces) Birds Eye
    Cauliflower
1 package (9 ounces) Birds Eye
    Whole Green Beans
1 package (10 ounces) Birds Eye
    Asparagus Spears
6 large carrots
4 stalks celery
2 medium tomatoes, sliced
2 to 4 slices Bermuda onion,
    separated into rings
Lettuce
Classic Bleu Cheese Dressing

In separate saucepans, cook frozen vegetables as directed on packages. Drain and chill. Meanwhile, cut carrots in half and cook until tender. Drain and chill. Cut celery into 3-inch pieces; cook until just tender. Drain and chill.

Arrange cooked vegetables, the tomatoes, and onion rings on lettuce. Serve with Classic Bleu Cheese Dressing. Makes 10 to 12 servings.

To make **Classic Bleu Cheese Dressing,** prepare 1 envelope Good Seasons Classic Salad Dressing Mix with vinegar, water, and oil as directed on envelope. Gradually add ½ cup sour cream, stirring constantly. Fold in ½ cup crumbled bleu cheese, mixing well. Makes 1¾ cups dressing.

PREPARE-AHEAD HINT. Cook vegetables, drain, and chill. Slice onion and wrap in foil. Wash lettuce and make dressing. Then assemble salad at meal-preparation time.

Patio Salad

Rice, peas, pickle, ham, and cheese strips mixed with mayonnaise. Small recipe serves 8, large recipe 36.

1 package (10 ounces) Birds Eye
  Green Peas
½ teaspoon salt
1½ cups water
1⅓ cups Minute Rice
½ cup chopped dill pickle
1 teaspoon grated onion
Dash of pepper
1 cup thin strips cooked ham
1 cup thin strips Swiss cheese
¾ cup mayonnaise

Add frozen peas and salt to water in saucepan. Bring quickly to a boil and boil 2 minutes. Then add Minute Rice. Mix just to moisten all rice. Cover, remove from heat, and let stand 5 minutes. Then stir in pickle, onion, and pepper. Mix lightly with a fork. Chill. Before serving, add ham, cheese, and mayonnaise, mixing lightly. Serve on crisp salad greens. Serves 8.

For party-size recipe (to serve 36), use the following:

5 packages (10 ounces each)
  Birds Eye Green Peas
2 to 3 teaspoons salt
2 quarts water
7 cups (23-⅛-ounce package)
  Minute Rice
3 cups mayonnaise mixed with 1
  to 1½ cups French dressing
2½ cups chopped dill pickles
2 tablespoons grated onion
¼ teaspoon pepper
1¼ quarts thin strips cooked ham
1¼ quarts thin strips Swiss cheese

Make as directed in recipe at left.
Oriental Patio Salad. Use small recipe for Patio Salad, but substitute 1 package (10 ounces) Birds Eye Peas and Carrots for the green peas; 1 cup cooked slivered chicken or turkey for the ham; add ⅔ cup (5-ounce can) drained water chestnuts, cut into thin strips, and omit the cheese.
PREPARE-AHEAD HINT. Fix salad but omit ham and cheese. Chill. Assemble salad at serving time.

Sunny Cream Cheese and Peach Salad (p. 46) needs no special mold to be festive. To decorate, pipe edges with whipped cream.

Cooked frozen green peas brighten all sorts of wonderful dishes. For this sprightly recipe, see Curried Vegetable Salad below.

Luncheon Salad

Cooked Lima beans, carrots, and beets, marinated in French dressing, and arranged with egg slices on lettuce.

1 package (10 ounces) Birds Eye
    Baby Lima Beans*
2 medium carrots — about 1 cup
    cooked and diced
2 medium beets — about 1 cup
    cooked and diced
½ cup French dressing
Lettuce
4 hard-cooked eggs, sliced
Paprika
Water cress

* Or use 1 package (10 ounces) Birds Eye Butter Beans or 1 package (9 ounces) Birds Eye Italian Green Beans.

Cook beans as directed on package. Drain. Cook carrots and beets. Drain and dice. Pour French dressing over vegetables and toss lightly. Chill. Spoon onto lettuce cups and arrange overlapping slices of egg across the top.

Sprinkle eggs with paprika. Garnish with water cress and mayonnaise or other salad dressing. Makes 4 servings.

Curried Vegetable Salad

Green peas and rice, flavored with curry and other seasonings and mixed with French dressing and mayonnaise.

1⅓ cups Minute Rice
1 teaspoon salt
1⅓ cups boiling water
¼ cup French dressing
¾ cup mayonnaise
1 tablespoon finely chopped onion
¾ teaspoon curry powder
⅛ teaspoon pepper
½ teaspoon dry mustard
1 tablespoon lemon juice
1 cup diced celery
1 package (10 ounces) Birds Eye
    Green Peas, cooked

Add Minute Rice and ½ teaspoon of

the salt to boiling water in saucepan. Mix just to moisten all rice. Cover and remove from heat. Let stand 5 minutes. Then uncover, add French dressing, mixing lightly; cool to room temperature.

About 1 hour before serving, combine mayonnaise, onion, curry powder, remaining ½ teaspoon salt, the pepper, dry mustard, and lemon juice, mixing well. Add to celery and peas in large bowl; then add rice, mixing lightly with a fork. Chill; serve on crisp lettuce. Makes about 5 or 6 servings.

For party-size recipe, use 4 cups Minute Rice and 2⅔ cups mayonnaise; triple all other ingredients. Serves 18.

PREPARE-AHEAD HINT. Make entire recipe ahead and allow time for ingredients to chill and flavors to blend.

Chilled and flavor-blended, Shrimp-Rice Salad (p. 49) makes a satisfying entrée for party luncheon or buffet. Serves 6 or 36.

Dessert emerges in a twinkling when you keep mixed fruit and sherbet on hand. At General Foods Kitchens we also enjoy this Summer Refresher (p. 56) made with ice cream.

Desserts

Desserts round out meals gracefully and leave a sense of well-being and satisfaction. Perhaps that's why women for generations have prized their dessert recipes and kept their special ones a family secret.

But there's always room for new fruit dessert recipes among the old favorites. Today with frozen foods we combine summer fruits with fall fruits and tropical flavors with northern flavors. We enjoy, for instance, the fresh-tasting flavor of frozen red raspberries with tree-ripened pears . . . or a lime snow with strawberries . . . or peaches with mincemeat. Popular standbys such as strawberry shortcake and rhubarb cobbler we now serve whenever the fancy strikes us, regardless of the season.

The desserts offered here run the gamut from simple-but-satisfying to slightly exotic. But even the most elaborate have been streamlined with the use of frozen foods.

GARNISHES

For almost any dessert — puddings, cakes, pies, berries, sliced fruits, or mixed fruits — garnish with a topping, sauce, ice cream, or sherbert.

Serve fruit pies with mint ice cream, or Dream Whip Dessert Topping or whipped cream, lightly sprinkled with grated nutmeg or chopped candied ginger.

For puddings and unfrosted cakes, fold drained, thawed, frozen berries or peaches into whipped cream or prepared Dream Whip Dessert Topping and use as a sauce or garnish.

Top plain cakes, fruit cobblers, fruit snows, and fruit turnovers with a lemon or orange sauce.

Serve berries, sliced fruits, or mixed fruits with a scoop of coffee or chocolate ice cream, lime or lemon sherbet, a sprinkling of Baker's Angel Flake Coconut, prepared Dream Whip Dessert Topping or whipped cream with curls of Baker's German's Sweet Chocolate.

Mixed Fruit Ambrosia

Suggested menu for three: Veal Roulades (p. 17), baked sweet potatoes, lettuce salad, and Ambrosia.

Empty 1 package (12 ounces) Birds Eye Mixed Fruit into a serving dish. Sprinkle with ½ cup Baker's Angel Flake Coconut. Let stand at room temperature until just thawed — about 2 hours. Mix lightly. Serves 3 or 4.

Fruit Medley. Cut melon balls from 1 cantaloupe and add to the mixed fruits.

Hawaiian Ambrosia. Add fresh pineapple, diced, to the mixed fruits.

Tropical Ambrosia. Add banana slices to the mixed fruits.

Summer Refresher

A simple but elegant dessert of mixed fruit and lime sherbet.

1 package (12 ounces) Birds Eye Mixed Fruit, just-thawed
1 pint lime sherbert

Spoon just-thawed fruit into sherbet glasses and top with a scoop of sherbet. Makes 4 servings.

Coconut Peach Melba

Peach halves covered with a thick- ened red raspberry sauce and sprinkled with snowy coconut.

1 package (10 ounces) Birds Eye
   Red Raspberries, thawed
2 teaspoons cornstarch
1 tablespoon sugar
Dash of salt
8 frozen peach halves,
   thawed and drained
1 cup Baker's Angel Flake Coconut

Drain raspberries, reserving juice. Com- bine cornstarch, sugar, and salt in a saucepan. Stir in ⅔ cup raspberry juice. Bring to a boil slowly, stirring constantly. Cook until mixture is clear, about 2. minutes. Cool slightly. Then fold in the drained raspberries. Chill. Serve over the peach halves and sprin- kle with coconut. Makes 4 servings.
PREPARE-AHEAD HINT. Make sauce and chill. Thaw peaches during meal- preparation. Assemble at serving time.

Peaches-in-Shells

Dessert shells made of frozen dessert topping and filled with frosty peaches.

1 envelope Dream Whip Dessert
   Topping Mix
½ cup milk
½ teaspoon vanilla
1 tablespoon grated orange rind
⅓ cup chopped nuts
2 packages (12 ounces each) Birds Eye
   Sliced Peaches, just-thawed

Prepare dessert topping mix with milk and vanilla as directed on the package. Fold in orange rind, blending well. Then fold in nuts. Drop mixture onto waxed paper, about ¼ cup at a time. With a spoon, make a depression in the top of each mound. Freeze until firm — 2 to 3 hours. Fill with peaches just before serving. Makes 9 servings.

PREPARE-AHEAD HINT. Make the nut shells and freeze as directed. Let peaches thaw during meal-preparation so that they're still icy-cold when served.

Peach Upside Down Cake

Company coming? Upside down cakes are always popular — and this one's so pretty, too.

1 package (12 ounces) Birds Eye
   Sliced Peaches, thawed
1 tablespoon lemon juice
½ cup butter
½ to ¾ cup firmly packed
   brown sugar
2 tablespoons flour
¼ cup slivered blanched almonds
¼ cup maraschino cherries, halved
1⅓ cups sifted Swans Down
   Cake Flour
2 teaspoons Calumet Baking Powder
¼ teaspoon salt
⅔ cup granulated sugar
⅓ cup milk
1 egg, unbeaten
1 teaspoon vanilla

Drain peaches, measuring ½ cup juice. Combine peaches and lemon juice and set aside. Place ¼ cup butter in 9-inch round cake pan. Heat in moderate oven (350°F.) until butter is melted. Com- bine brown sugar, flour, and ½ cup peach juice. Stir into the melted butter. Arrange peach slices, slivered almonds, and cherries in butter mixture.

Measure sifted flour, add baking powder, salt, and granulated sugar, and sift together. Cream remaining ¼ cup butter until softened. Add dry ingre- dients, milk, egg, and vanilla. Stir to moisten all the flour; then beat vigor- ously 1 minute. Pour over fruit mix- ture in pan. Bake in moderate oven (350°F.) about 45 minutes, or until cake springs back when pressed lightly. Cool about 5 minutes. Invert onto serving plate and let stand 1 minute before removing pan. Serve warm or cold. Top each serving with whipped cream or prepared Dream Whip Dessert Topping or ice cream, if desired. Makes about 8 servings.

PREPARE-AHEAD HINT. Make ahead and serve cold or reheat in slow oven just until slightly warm.

Raspberry-Glazed Cheesecake

Another favorite of General Foods Kitchens and a perfect finish for a light party meal.

⅓ cup graham cracker crumbs
⅓ cup zwieback crumbs
2 tablespoons sugar
⅛ teaspoon cinnamon
3 tablespoons butter, melted
3 packages (8 ounces each)
  cream cheese
3 eggs, slightly beaten
¾ cup sugar
⅛ teaspoon salt
1 tablespoon lemon juice
1 teaspoon vanilla
Raspberry Glaze

Combine crumbs, 2 tablespoons sugar, and the cinnamon. Add melted butter and mix until evenly distributed. Heavily grease a 9-inch spring-form pan on bottom and sides. Sprinkle ¼ cup of the crumb mixture around sides of the pan. Press remaining crumb mixture in bottom of pan.

Beat cream cheese until thoroughly softened. Add eggs, a little at a time, beating after each addition until smooth. Add remaining sugar, the salt, lemon juice, and vanilla. Beat thoroughly until sugar is dissolved.

Pour filling into crumb-lined pan. Bake in a hot oven (425°F.) for 20 minutes, or until top is set and lightly browned. (Center will be soft but sets up as it cools.) Chill at least 4 hours. Then pour Raspberry Glaze over top.

Chill until set. To store, keep in refrigerator. Makes 8 to 12 servings.

*To Make **Raspberry Glaze**,* partly thaw 1 package (10 ounces) Birds Eye Red Raspberries. Soften 2 teaspoons gelatin in 2 tablespoons cold water. Press raspberries through a sieve or ricer. Or blend berries until smooth in an electric blender and strain. Discard seeds. Place purée in a saucepan and bring to a boil. Remove from heat and add gelatin, stirring until dissolved. Chill until slightly thickened before pouring over cheesecake.

Strawberry Shortcake

Deliciously different, this shortcake is made with rounds of shortbread, ice cream, and berries.

½ cup soft butter
¼ cup sugar
1¼ cups sifted flour
1 quart vanilla ice cream,
  slightly softened
2 packages (1 pound each) Birds Eye
  Sliced Strawberries, just-thawed*

* Or use 3 packages (10 ounces each) Birds Eye Strawberry Halves.

Mix butter and sugar with pastry blender or fork. Add flour and mix until crumbs are formed. Then mix gently but thoroughly until soft dough is formed. Roll ¼ inch thick on lightly floured board. Cut into 16 rounds with floured 2½-inch cooky cutter. Place rounds on baking sheet and prick tops several times with a fork. Bake in a slow oven (325°F.) about 35 minutes, or until lightly browned. Cool.

Place a shortbread round in each dessert nappy. Top with a medium scoop of ice cream; flatten ice cream slightly. Spoon half the strawberries and juice over ice cream. Top with another shortbread round, another scoop of ice cream, and garnish with remaining strawberries and juice. Serves 8.

PREPARE-AHEAD HINT. Make pastry

rounds. Let berries thaw during meal preparation. Berries should be icy cold when served. Assemble at serving time.

Rainbow Tea Cakes

Dainty cupcakes — about the size of a large thimble — frosted in many pastel colors.

2 packages Swans Down
    Yellow Cake Mix
2½ cups water
4 eggs, unbeaten
Orange Cream Cheese Frosting (p. 80)
Pink Cream Cheese Frosting (p. 80)
Lime Cream Cheese Frosting (p. 80)

Prepare each package of cake mix with 1¼ cups water and 2 eggs as directed on package. Set paper liners in 1-inch cupcake pans. Fill about two-thirds full. Bake in moderate oven (350°F.) for 20 to 25 minutes. Cool.

Frost a third of the cupcakes with the orange frosting, another third with the pink frosting, and remaining cupcakes with the lime frosting. Use about 1½ teaspoons frosting on each cupcake. Makes about 180 frosted cakes. *Note:* If desired, make half the recipe for each of these cream cheese frostings, (p. 80): Orange or Tangerine, Pink, Lemon, Lime, and Grape. Frost a fifth of the cakes with each.

No juice to squeeze, no rind to grate when you make Lemon Meringue Pie with concentrated lemonade. For recipe, see p. 63.

Rhubarb Cobbler

Especially good served warm with a dollop of hard sauce or whipped cream, a fluffy sauce or plain light cream.

1 cup sifted flour
2 teaspoons Calumet Baking Powder
¼ teaspoon salt
¼ teaspoon cream of tartar
1 tablespoon sugar
¼ cup shortening
⅓ cup milk
2 packages (1 pound each)
  Birds Eye Rhubarb, thawed
2 tablespoons Minute Tapioca
½ to ¾ cup sugar
1 tablespoon lemon juice
⅛ teaspoon nutmeg
⅛ teaspoon almond extract
2 drops red food coloring (optional)
1 tablespoon butter

Measure sifted flour, add baking powder, salt, cream of tartar, and sugar and sift again. Cut in shortening until mixture resembles coarse crumbs. Add milk and stir with fork until soft dough is formed. Turn out on lightly floured board and pat or roll lightly to fit top of a 1½-quart baking dish. Cut several slits near center of dough.

Combine rhubarb, Minute Tapioca, sugar, lemon juice, and nutmeg in saucepan. Cook and stir until mixture comes to a full boil. Add almond extract and food coloring. Pour into greased 1½-quart baking dish. Dot with butter. Adjust dough over hot fruit mixture, sealing edges and opening slits to permit steam to escape. Bake in hot oven (400°F.) for 25 to 30 minutes, or until biscuit topping is lightly browned. Makes 6 to 8 servings.

Strawberry-Rhubarb Cobbler. Use above recipe but substitute 1 package (10 ounces) Birds Eye Sliced Strawberries or Strawberry Halves for one package of the rhubarb. Reduce Minute Tapioca to 1½ tablespoons and sugar to ¼ cup. Makes 6 to 8 servings.

PREPARE-AHEAD HINT. Make cobbler ahead and reheat in oven at serving time just long enough to warm slightly.

Blueberry Cottage Pudding

A clear, rosy sauce made with tropical juices and served over blueberry pudding. Luscious!

1½ cups sifted flour
1½ teaspoons Calumet
  Baking Powder
¼ teaspoon salt
1½ cups blueberries
2 tablespoons sifted flour
⅓ cup butter, softened
¾ cup sugar
1 egg
½ cup light cream
Tropical Sauce

Measure 1½ cups sifted flour, add baking powder and salt, and sift together. Gently mix blueberries in a bowl with 2 tablespoons flour; set aside.

Cream butter and sugar together thoroughly. Add egg and beat until mixture is very light and fluffy. Blend in cream; then add sifted dry ingredients and beat just until mixed. Fold in floured blueberries. Pour into a greased 9x9x2-inch pan. Bake in a moderate oven (350°F.) 30 to 35 minutes. Serve warm and top with hot sauce. Makes 9 servings.

*To make **Tropical Sauce,*** combine ½ cup sugar, 2 tablespoons cornstarch, ⅛ teaspoon ground cloves, and dash salt in saucepan. Add 1 cup water, stirring constantly. Then add ½ cup Birds Eye Concentrated Chill-Ripe Punch. Cook and stir over medium heat until thick and clear, about 5 minutes. Remove from heat. Add 1 tablepsoon butter; blend well. Makes about 1⅓ cups sauce.

PREPARE-AHEAD HINT. Make pudding and sauce. At meal-preparation time, warm pudding in slow oven. Reheat sauce just until hot.

60

Miracle Strawberry Pie

Strawberries and crushed pineapple in a clear, thickened filling.

1 package (10 ounces) Birds Eye
    Sliced Strawberries or Strawberry
    Halves, thawed
1 can (8 ounces) crushed pineapple
¼ teaspoon salt
2 teaspoons lemon juice
1 package Jell-O Vanilla Pudding
    and Pie Filling
1 tablespoon butter
1 baked 8-inch pie shell, cooled
½ cup whipping cream*

* Or use 1 cup prepared Dream Whip Dessert Topping.

In a medium saucepan, combine strawberries, pineapple, salt, lemon juice, and pudding mix. Cook and stir over medium heat until mixture comes to a *full* boil, about 5 minutes. Remove from heat. Add butter. Cool 5 minutes, stirring once or twice. Pour into pie shell and let stand about 3 hours, or until firm. Before serving, whip cream and spread over pie.

PREPARE-AHEAD HINT. Make pie as directed. While filling is still warm, cover surface with waxed paper to avoid formation of a film. Just before serving, remove waxed paper. Whip cream and spread over pie.

Crisscross Pie

Peaches, cherries, berries, and grapes, baked in a shell with a lattice top crust.

2 tablespoons Minute Tapioca
¼ cup sugar
¼ teaspoon cinnamon
¼ teaspoon salt
1 package (12 ounces) Birds Eye
    Mixed Fruit, thawed
1 package (12 ounces) Birds Eye
    Sliced Peaches, thawed
1 tablespoon lemon juice
Pastry for 8-inch pie
1 tablespoon butter

Combine Minute Tapioca, sugar, cinnamon, salt, undrained fruits, and lemon juice. Let stand 15 minutes.

Use half of pastry for bottom crust. Roll ⅛ inch thick. Fit into an 8-inch pie shell and trim edges. Moisten edge of crust. Roll remaining pastry ⅛ inch thick and about an inch larger than top of pie pan. Then cut into strips about ½ inch wide.

Spoon filling into pie shell. Dot with butter. Arrange half of the strips in rows about an inch apart across the filling. Then place remaining strips across the first rows at an angle to form squares or diamond shapes. Fold ends of strips under bottom crust. Press together with fingers or fork.

Bake in hot oven (425°F.) for 35 to 40 minutes, or until syrup boils with heavy bubbles that do not burst.

Strawberry-Rhubarb Pie

Suggested menu: Roast lamb, Vegetable Supreme (p. 34), leaf lettuce salad, and Strawberry-Rhubarb Pie.

Pastry for two-crust 9-inch pie
1 package (1 pound) Birds Eye
    Rhubarb, thawed
1 package (10 ounces) Birds Eye
    Sliced Strawberries or Strawberry
    Halves, thawed
½ cup sugar
3 tablespoons cornstarch
    or 4 tablespoons flour
2 tablespoons butter

Use half of pastry for bottom crust; roll ⅛ inch thick. Fit into a 9-inch pie pan and trim edges. For top crust, roll remaining pastry ⅛ inch thick and cut several 2-inch slits near center.

Combine fruits and pour into pie shell. Mix sugar and cornstarch or flour and sprinkle on fruits. Dot with butter. Moisten edge of bottom crust.

Fold top crust in half or roll loosely on rolling pin to lift and center on filling. Open slits to let steam escape during baking. Trim top crust ½ inch larger than pan. Fold edge of top crust under bottom crust and press together.

Bake in hot oven (425°F.) for 45 minutes, or until syrup boils with heavy bubbles that do not burst.

Raspberry Bavarian Pie

Lemon-flavored gelatin with whipped cream and raspberries folded in; serve in your favorite pie shell.

2 packages (10 ounces each) Birds Eye
    Red Raspberries, thawed
⅓ cup raspberry juice and water
1 regular size package (3 ounces)
    Lemon Jell-O Gelatin
1 cup boiling water
¼ cup sugar
Dash of salt
2 tablespoons lemon juice
1 cup whipping cream*
1 baked 9-inch pie shell, cooled

* Or use 1 envelope Dream Whip Dessert Topping Mix and prepare as directed on package.

Thaw raspberries. Add water to juice to make ⅓ cup. Dissolve Jell-O in boiling water. Add diluted raspberry juice, sugar, salt, and lemon juice. Chill until slightly thickened. Whip cream. Then fold raspberries and cream into Jell-O. Pour into cooled baked pie shell. Chill until firm.

Peach-Mincemeat Pie

Suggested menu: hot Vegetable Blender Soup (p. 2), ham salad, relishes, hot rolls, and Peach-Mincemeat Pie.

2 packages (12 ounces each) Birds Eye
    Sliced Peaches, thawed
¾ cup peach juice
1½ cups moist mincemeat
2 tablespoons Minute Tapioca
3 tablespoons sugar
¼ teaspoon salt
2 tablespoons lemon juice
Pastry for a two-crust 9-inch pie

Drain and dice peaches. Then combine peaches, ¾ cup of the peach juice, the mincemeat, tapioca, sugar, salt, and lemon juice in a bowl. Let stand about 15 minutes.

Use half of pastry for bottom crust; roll ⅛ inch thick. Fit into a 9-inch pie pan and trim edges. For top crust, roll remaining pastry ⅛ inch thick and cut several 2-inch slits near center.

Pour filling into pie shell. Moisten edge of bottom crust. Fold top crust in half or roll loosely on rolling pin to lift and center on filling. Open slits to let steam escape during baking. Trim top crust ½ inch larger than pan. Fold edge of top crust under bottom crust and press together.

Bake in hot oven (425°F.) for 45 minutes, or until syrup boils with heavy bubbles that do not burst.

Miracle Peach Pie

Suggested menu: Broiled Fish with Cucumber Sauce (p. 26), crinkle-cut French fried potatoes, green beans, and Miracle Peach Pie.

1 package (12 ounces) Birds Eye
    Sliced Peaches, slightly thawed
1¼ cups water
1 package Jell-O Vanilla Pudding
    and Pie Filling
¼ teaspoon salt
2 teaspoons lemon juice
1 tablespoon butter
¼ teaspoon almond extract
1 baked 8-inch pie shell, cooled
Sweetened whipped cream or
    prepared Dream Whip
    Dessert Topping

Cut slightly thawed peaches into bite-size pieces. Add to ½ cup of the water in a saucepan. Bring to a boil. Meanwhile, combine pudding mix, salt, lemon juice, and remaining ¾ cup water. Stir to form a smooth paste. Add to boiling fruit, stirring to blend.

Then cook and stir until mixture comes to a *full* boil.

Remove from heat and add butter and almond extract. Cool 5 minutes, stirring once or twice. Pour into pie shell. Let stand about 3 hours, or until firm. Serve with whipped cream.

PREPARE-AHEAD HINT. Make pie as directed. While filling is still warm, cover surface with waxed paper to avoid formation of a film. Just before serving, remove waxed paper. Whip cream and spread over top of pie.

Summer and fall flavors blend in this scrumptious pie of frozen red raspberries and tart apples. Recipe on p. 64.

Lemon Meringue Pie

Suggested menu: Chicken Cosmopolitan (p. 20), large tossed salad, and Lemon Meringue Pie.

6 tablespoons cornstarch
1 cup sugar
¼ teaspoon salt
2 cups water
3 egg yolks, slightly beaten
2 tablespoons butter
½ cup Birds Eye Concentrated Lemonade
1 baked 9-inch pie shell
3 egg whites
6 tablespoons sugar

Combine cornstarch, 1 cup sugar, and salt in top of double boiler. Add water gradually, blending well. Cook and stir over boiling water until mixture is thickened and clear. Then cover and cook 15 minutes longer. Remove from boiling water; add gradually to egg yolks, stirring constantly. Return to top of double boiler. Cook and stir over boiling water 3 minutes longer. Remove from boiling water, add butter and concentrated lemonade, and blend. Cool only about 5 minutes, stirring once or twice. Pour into baked pie shell.

Beat egg whites until foamy throughout. Add remaining sugar, 2 tablespoons at a time, beating after each addition until sugar is blended. Then continue beating until meringue stands in peaks. Spread over pie filling. Bake in hot oven (425°F.) 5 minutes, or until meringue is lightly browned.

Quick Fruited Gelatin

Fix an hour before dinner and this dessert will be ready at dessert time.

1 family size package (6 ounces) Raspberry Jell-O Gelatin*
2 cups boiling water
2 packages (10 ounces each) Birds Eye Red Raspberries
1 cup cold water
2 bananas, thinly sliced

* Or use 2 regular size packages (3 ounces each) Raspberry Jell-O Gelatin.

Dissolve Jell-O in boiling water. Add frozen blocks of raspberries and the cold water. Stir until fruit is thawed and Jell-O is slightly thickened. Fold in banana. Pour into serving dishes or a 2-quart mold. Chill until firm. Serve with cream, if desired. Serves 12.

Double Strawberry. Follow above recipe, but substitute Strawberry Jell-O Gelatin for the raspberry flavor and 2 packages (10 ounces each) Birds Eye Sliced Strawberries or Strawberry Halves for the red raspberries.

Peach-and-Lemon. Use recipe for Quick Fruited Gelatin (p. 63), but substitute Lemon Jell-O Gelatin for the raspberry flavor and 2 packages (12 ounces each) Birds Eye Sliced Peaches for the red raspberries.

Jellied Medley. Use recipe for Quick Fruited Gelatin (p. 63), but substitute Cherry Jell-O Gelatin for the raspberry flavor and 2 packages (12 ounces each) Birds Eye Mixed Fruit for the red raspberries.

Raspberry-Apple Pie

Summer and fall flavors blend in this scrumptious pie. If your family insists on pie with trimmings, serve this á la mode or with cheese.

¼ cup Minute Tapioca
½ cup sugar
½ teaspoon salt
2 packages (10 ounces each) Birds Eye
   Red Raspberries, thawed
2 cups sliced peeled apples
1 tablespoon lemon juice
¼ teaspoon nutmeg
Pastry for a two-crust 9-inch pie
2 tablespoons butter

Combine Minute Tapioca, sugar, salt, fruits, lemon juice, and nutmeg. Let stand about 15 minutes.

Use half the pastry for bottom crust. Roll ⅛ inch thick. Fit into a 9-inch pie pan and trim edges. For top crust, roll remaining pastry ⅛ inch thick and cut several 2-inch slits near center. Spoon filling into pie shell. Dot with butter. Moisten edges of bottom crust.

Fold top crust in half or roll loosely on rolling pin to lift and center on filling. Open slits to let steam escape during baking. Trim top crust ½ inch larger than pan. Fold edge under bottom crust and press together.

Bake in hot oven (425°F.) 60 to 65 minutes, or until syrup boils with heavy bubbles that do not burst.

Ambassador Strawberry Tarts

This filling is too soft for a pie but luscious in tart shells.

1 egg white
¼ cup sugar
½ cup whipping cream*
½ teaspoon vanilla
1⅓ cups (about) Baker's Angel
   Flake Coconut
1 package (10 ounces) Birds Eye
   Sliced Strawberries or
   Strawberry Halves, thawed
5 baked 3½-inch tart shells, cooled

* Or use 1 cup prepared Dream Whip Dessert Topping.

Beat egg white until foamy throughout. Add sugar, 2 tablespoons at a time, beating after each addition until sugar is blended. Then continue beating until mixture will stand in peaks. Whip cream, add vanilla, and fold into meringue mixture. Add 1 cup of the coconut. Place strawberries in tart shells and top with the cream mixture. Sprinkle with remaining coconut. Serve at once. Makes 5 tarts.

For tart shells, use a pastry mix or any favorite recipe (enough for about 1 pie crust). Roll ⅛ inch thick. Cut five 6-inch rounds of pastry. Fit carefully over outside of tart or muffin pans. Bake in hot oven (450°F.) for 12 to 15 minutes, or until lightly browned.

For 6 to 8 tarts, use a 1-pound package of Birds Eye Sliced Strawberries.

Ambassador Raspberry Tarts. Use above recipe but substitute 1 package (10 ounces) Birds Eye Red Raspberries for the strawberries.

Ambassador Peach Tarts. Use above recipe but substitute 1 package (12 ounces) Birds Eye Sliced Peaches for the strawberries.

PREPARE-AHEAD HINT. Bake tart shells. Make filling at meal-preparation time.

Ginger Orange Whip

Suggested menu: Smothered Chicken (p. 20), sliced tomato, cucumber, and onion salad, hot biscuits, beverage, and Ginger Orange Whip.

1 regular size package (3 ounces)
  Orange Jell-O Gelatin
1 cup hot ginger ale
1 cup reconstituted Birds Eye
  Orange Juice
Sweetened whipped cream or prepared
  Dream Whip Dessert Topping
Chopped candied ginger (optional)

Dissolve Jell-O in *hot* ginger ale. Add orange juice. Chill until slightly thickened. Then place bowl of Jell-O in ice and water and whip with egg beater until fluffy and thick. Spoon into 1-quart ring mold. Chill until firm. Unmold. Fill center of mold with sweetened whipped cream and sprinkle with chopped candied ginger, if desired. Makes 4 to 6 servings.

Pastel Snow

A special favorite of General Foods Kitchens . . . delicate and airy with refreshing fruit flavor.

1 envelope (1 tablespoon) gelatin
½ cup sugar
¼ teaspoon salt
1¼ cups hot water
1 can (6 ounces) Birds Eye Concentrated
  Orange Juice, thawed*
2 egg whites, unbeaten
Custard Sauce

* Or use Concentrated Limeade, Lemonade, Concord Grape Juice, Grapefruit Juice, Tangerine Juice, Orange and Grapefruit Juice, or Chill-Ripe Punch.

Combine gelatin, sugar, and salt. Add hot water and stir until gelatin is dissolved. Add concentrated orange juice and blend well. Chill until slightly thickened. Then place in bowl of ice and water, add unbeaten egg whites, and beat with electric beater or sturdy egg beater until mixture forms soft peaks. Pour into 1½-quart mold or 8 individual molds. Chill until firm. Unmold. Serve with sauce. Serves 8.

*To make **Custard Sauce**,* beat 2 egg yolks slightly. Combine with 2 tablespoons sugar and 1½ cups milk in top of double boiler. Cook and stir over hot water until mixture is thickened and coats a dry metal spoon. Cool. Add ½ teaspoon vanilla. Chill, if desired. Makes 1½ cups sauce.

Angel Pudding

A Bavarian-type dessert, garnished with strawberries or red raspberries.

1 envelope (1 tablespoon) gelatin
¼ cup cold water
¾ cup boiling water
1 can (6 ounces) Birds Eye
  Concentrated Lemonade, thawed*
½ cup sugar
1 cup whipping cream or 1 envelope
  Dream Whip Dessert Topping Mix
1 package (10 ounces) Birds Eye
  Sliced Strawberries, Strawberry
  Halves, or Red Raspberries

* Or use 1 can (6 ounces) Birds Eye Concentrated Limeade, Chill-Ripe Punch, or Concord Grape Juice.

Sprinkle gelatin on cold water. When gelatin has absorbed the water, add boiling water and stir until gelatin is dissolved. Add concentrated lemonade and sugar; mix well. Chill until gelatin is slightly thickened.

Whip with egg beater or electric mixer until thick and fluffy. Whip cream. Fold into whipped gelatin mixture. Pour into individual serving dishes. Chill until firm, about 2 hours. Top each serving with about a tablespoon of berries or garnish with a mint leaf or maraschino cherry, if desired. Makes 8 to 10 servings.

As luscious as it looks, this favorite has a filling of juicy mixed fruits. The recipe? See Crisscross Pie (p. 61).

Lemon Sponge Pudding

A delicate fruit-flavored pudding that forms a sponge-cake top and custard sauce as pudding bakes.

2 tablespoons butter
1 cup sugar
4 egg yolks, unbeaten
½ cup Birds Eye Concentrated
  Lemonade*
¼ teaspoon salt
2 tablespoons flour
1 cup milk
4 egg whites, stiffly beaten

* Or use ½ cup Birds Eye Concentrated Orange Juice or Limeade.

Cream butter, add sugar gradually, and cream together until light and fluffy. Add egg yolks and beat well. Then add concentrated lemonade and salt; blend.

Add flour and milk, mixing well. Fold in beaten egg whites, blending well. Pour into greased custard cups. Place in pan of hot water and bake in moderate oven (375°F.) for 25 minutes. Chill, if desired. Unmold and garnish with whipped cream. Makes 8 servings. **PREPARE-AHEAD HINT.** Bake pudding and serve chilled, if desired.

Coeur á la Creme

Chill in a heart-shaped mold for Valentine's Day, engagement or anniversary parties, or wedding showers.

2 teaspoons gelatin
3 tablespoons cold water
1 pound (2 cups) cottage cheese
2 packages (3 ounces each)
  cream cheese
1 cup heavy cream
1 tablespoon confectioners' sugar
3 packages (10 ounces each) Birds Eye
  Sliced Strawberries or Strawberry
  Halves, just-thawed

Soften gelatin in cold water. Heat over

Destined for oohs and ahs is angel food cake made from a Swans Down mix and served with frosty strawberries.

hot water until dissolved. Put cottage cheese through a fine sieve. Soften cream cheese; add cream gradually, blending well. Add sugar and the cottage cheese. Stir in dissolved gelatin. Spoon into 1-quart mold or individual molds. Chill until firm. Unmold. Top with the sliced strawberries. Makes 8 to 10 servings. **PREPARE-AHEAD HINT.** Make dessert and chill as directed. Thaw berries while preparing meal.

Strawberry-Filled Dessert Pancakes

Delicate, lightly spiced pancakes, folded and then filled with berries.

2 tablespoons sugar
½ teaspoon ground cardamon seeds
   or ¼ teaspoon nutmeg
1½ cups pancake mix
4 eggs, well beaten
1⅔ cups milk
½ cup melted butter
2 packages (1 pound each) Birds Eye
   Whole Strawberries, thawed
   and drained*
Confectioners' sugar

* Or use General Foods Kitchens Strawberry-Cherry Jam (see recipe on p. 88).

Add sugar and spice to pancake mix; stir lightly. Combine eggs, milk, and butter. Gradually add the pancake mix, beating until smooth. Pour batter onto a hot ungreased griddle, spreading quickly to form thin 6-inch pancakes. Bake until bubbles form across top; then turn and bake on other side.

As pancakes are removed from the griddle, fold in half; then in half again to form triangles. Place on wire cake rack. Fill top and bottom folds with strawberries or with Strawberry-Cherry

Jam. Then place in slow oven (300°F.) to keep hot until ready to serve. Sprinkle with confectioners' sugar. Makes about 2 dozen 6-inch pancakes, or enough for 6 to 8 servings. **PREPARE-AHEAD HINT.** Thaw berries in packages. Measure and combine dry ingredients. Combine eggs and milk and refrigerate. Mix batter at meal-preparation time, adding melted butter, and proceed with recipe.

Pilgrim Cups

If you like pumpkin pie, you'll also like this squash dessert with a brown-sugar-and-butter topping.

1 package (12 ounces) Birds Eye
   Cooked Squash, thawed
3 eggs, slightly beaten
½ cup sugar
¾ teaspoon salt
¾ teaspoon grated orange rind
¾ teaspoon cinnamon
2¼ cups milk
Praline Topping

Combine squash, eggs, sugar, salt, orange rind, and cinnamon. Add milk gradually and mix well. Pour into greased custard cups. Place in pan of hot water and bake in moderate oven (375°F.) for 35 minutes, or until set. Spread with Praline Topping and bake 10 minutes more, or until topping bubbles. Serve warm or chilled. Serves 9. *To make* **Praline Topping,** *mix* ⅓ cup firmly packed brown sugar with 1 tablespoon flour. Blend in 3 tablespoons melted butter and 1 tablespoon water. Add ⅓ cup finely chopped nuts; mix well. Spread carefully, a small amount at a time, over custards; then bake.

To glorify a holiday fruit punch, wreathe rim of bowl with unsweetened whipped cream, lightly tinted and decorated with sprigs of mint. For other punch garnishes, see p. 70.

SECTION 6

GENERAL FOODS
KITCHENS

Fruit Drinks

Mention fruit drinks and you think of social times and leisure moments —
bridge parties, graduation or engagement teas, proms, picnics in the backyard, or an after-shopping pause when mother and daughter relax together
on a hot Saturday. Fruit drinks are truly refreshment.

With so many frozen fruit juices on the market, there's no end to the
flavor blends you can concoct. We've given you a sampling of recipes to
suit different size groups. These are adaptable recipes that you can vary, if
you please, or use as a guide for developing others specially your own.
One caution: When experimenting with mixing fruit juices, try a small
amount first to see what color changes take place. You want colors clear
and sparkling. And remember to serve fruit drinks frosty cold.

GARNISHES

For fruit drinks served in glasses, use mint sprigs; a thin slice of orange,
slit and perched on the rim of the glass; floating banana slices, maraschino cherries; or whole berries.

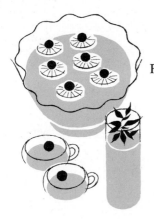

For punch bowls, float banana, orange, lemon, or lime slices. Or add an entire block of frozen berries, fruit-juice ice cubes, or rings made of reconstituted fruit juices, frozen in small ring molds. (These are especially attractive with maraschino cherries set in each ice cube or at intervals around the rings before freezing.)

Orange Frosted

Serve with tea cakes or cookies to bridge or canasta club or members of the senior dance committee.

1 can (6 ounces) Birds Eye Concentrated
   Orange Juice*
3 cans cold water
1 pint vanilla ice cream

* Or use Birds Eye Concentrated Concord Grape Juice, Tangerine Juice, or Chill-Ripe Punch.

Mix concentrated fruit juice with water. Add ice cream. Beat 1 minute with egg beater or in electric blender. Serve in tall glasses. Makes 6 to 8 servings.

Grape Sparkler

A tangy drink for TV nights or teen-age platter parties.

1 can (6 ounces) Birds Eye Concentrated
   Concord Grape Juice
2¼ cups chilled ginger ale

Combine grape juice and ginger ale. Mix well. Makes about 3 cups, or 6 four-ounce servings.
Orange Sparkler. Use above recipe but substitute Birds Eye Concentrated Orange Juice for the grape juice and increase ginger ale to 3 cups.

Lemon Soft Drink

When the gang gathers after school, let them make their own favorite fruit-juice beverage.

2 or 3 tablespoons Birds Eye
   Concentrated Lemonade,
   partly thawed
1 bottle (8 ounces) root beer*
Ice cubes

* Or use 1 bottle (6 or 8 ounces) cola beverage.

Combine ingredients in tall glass and serve. Makes 1 serving.
Lime Soft Drink. Use above recipe but substitute Birds Eye Concentrated Limeade for the lemonade.

Harvest Mist

Crushed lemonade ice and grape juice, decorated with mint leaves, and sipped through a straw.

1 can (6 ounces) Birds Eye Concentrated
   Lemonade, partly thawed
4⅓ cans (about) cold water
1 can (6 ounces) Birds Eye Concentrated
   Concord Grape Juice, partly thawed
3 cans cold water
Fresh mint leaves

Mix concentrated lemonade with about 4⅓ cans cold water. Blend well and pour into two ice cube trays. Freeze.

Mix concentrated grape juice with 3 cans cold water and chill. When ready to serve, crush the lemonade ice cubes and place in sherbet glasses. Pour the chilled grape juice over the lemonade ice. Garnish with fresh mint leaves and serve with short straws. Makes 6 servings.

Tropical Mist. Use above recipe but substitute 1 can (6 ounces) Birds Eye Concentrated Chill-Ripe Punch for the lemonade and 1 can (6 ounces) Birds Eye Concentrated Orange Juice or Lemonade for the grape juice.

PREPARE-AHEAD HINT. Fix fruit-ice cubes, allowing plenty of time to freeze. Mix remaining concentrate with water. Chill until ready to use.

Float a block of frozen fruit on any cold punch for garnish. It's colorful, cooling, and best of all, it's deliciously edible.

Every party needs good mixers such as the frozen concentrates in Tea Punch (p. 74). Add joyous touch with fanciful garnish.

Fruit Zip

A quick refresher for a hot day. Recipe makes a single serving.

2 tablespoons Birds Eye Concentrated
   Limeade, partly thawed*
2 or 3 ice cubes
Quinine water or lemon-lime
   carbonated beverage

* Or use Birds Eye Concentrated Tangerine Juice,
Orange and Grapefruit Juice, Grapefruit Juice,
Lemonade, Orange Juice, or Concord Grape Juice.

Spoon concentrated limeade (right from the can) into a tall glass. Add ice cubes and fill with quinine water or lemon-lime carbonated beverage. Stir to mix well. Makes 1 serving.

Tropical Pink Limeade

The tropical juices of Chill-Ripe Punch blended with limeade. Makes 8 five-ounce servings.

1 can (6 ounces) Birds Eye Concentrated
   Limeade
5 cans water
1 can (6 ounces) Birds Eye Concentrated
   Chill-Ripe Punch
Mint leaves (optional)

Combine concentrated limeade, water, and concentrated punch, mixing well. Pour over ice in glasses. Garnish with mint leaves, if desired. Makes about 8 five-ounce servings.

72

PREPARE-AHEAD HINT. Punch may be made well in advance and kept chilled.

Pink Punch

An intriguing punch of fruit juices with a touch of bitters and floating fruit-ice cubes. Makes 24 four-ounce servings.

2 cans (6 ounces each) Birds Eye
   Concentrated Lemonade
1 can (6 ounces) Birds Eye Concentrated
   Orange Juice
Water
Maraschino cherries
½ teaspoon bitters
2 tablespoons maraschino cherry juice

Mix 1 can of concentrated lemonade and 1 can of concentrated orange juice with water as directed on the cans. Pour juices separately into ice cube trays, setting aside any juice that is left over. Place a maraschino cherry in each cube. Freeze until firm.

About 15 minutes before serving, mix second can of lemonade with cold water as directed on can. Add any left-over lemonade and orange juice, the bitters, and cherry juice. Serve with the fruit-ice cubes. Makes about 3 quarts, or about 24 servings.

PREPARE-AHEAD HINT. Fix fruit-ice cubes the night before. Rest of punch may also be made ahead and kept chilled, if desired.

Punches needn't wait for parties. When you stock frozen juices in the freezer, anytime at all is the time for refreshment.

When a hot sun casts leaf shadows on the wall, serve Fruit Zip (p. 72) — a cool blend of your favorite juice and quinine water.

Strawberry Punch

A most pleasant punch made in a blender. Makes 12 four-ounce servings.

1 package (10 ounces) Birds Eye
  Sliced Strawberries or Strawberry
  Halves, partly thawed*
1 can (6 ounces) Birds Eye
  Chill-Ripe Punch
2 cups water
2 bottles (7 ounces each) club soda
Ice cubes

* Or use 1 package (10 ounces) Birds Eye Red Raspberries or 1 package (12 ounces) Birds Eye Frozen Peaches.

Place strawberry halves in blender and blend until smooth. Combine Chill-Ripe Punch, water, and puréed strawberries. Just before serving, add club soda and ice cubes. Makes about 6 cups, or 12 four-ounce servings.

PREPARE-AHEAD HINT. Make punch but omit soda and ice cubes. Chill soda; add with ice cubes just before serving.

Tea Punch

Iced tea with lemonade, limeade, cranberry juice, and ginger ale. Makes 40 four-ounce servings.

1 quart water
¼ cup loose tea*
1 quart cold water
2 cans (6 ounces each) Birds Eye
  Concentrated Lemonade
2 cans (6 ounces each) Birds Eye
  Concentrated Limeade
1 bottle (2 cups) cranberry juice
  cocktail
2 bottles (28 ounces each) ginger ale

* Or use 12 tea bags.

74

Bring water to a boil in saucepan. Remove from heat and immediately add the tea. Cover and brew 4 minutes; stir. Meanwhile, place cold water in punch bowl. Strain tea into punch bowl and then stir in concentrates and cranberry juice cocktail. Add ginger ale and ice just before serving. Makes about 5 quarts, or 40 four-ounce servings.

PREPARE-AHEAD HINT. Make punch, omitting the ginger ale. Chill and add ginger ale just before serving.

There's an air of gaiety in the house when the punch bowl graces the table. Note ice cubes made with frozen fruit juice.

Even dawdlers pick up appetite and finish meals on schedule when Mom promises to serve a Silken Sauce (p. 82) over ice cream. Try also on mixed fruits, gelatin whips, and puddings.

Delicious This-and-That

Most of us expect more than nourishment from our food — (though, of course, nourishment is important). We anticipate the pleasure of eating, and now and then look for something a little different to lift the spirits.

Among the recipes that follow are frostings in rainbow hues, salad dressings with just the right tartness for fruits, orange butters for vegetables, unusual stuffings and sauces, easy-glazed muffins, and curried fruits.

Here, too, are other meal brighteners suggested by General Foods Kitchens.

GARNISHES FOR FROSTINGS

Decorate sides and a border around rim of frosted cake with pecan or walnut halves, sliced Brazil nuts, or slivered toasted almonds. Or dribble frosting with a glaze made by melting 1 square chocolate with 1 teaspoon butter.

Make a border around top only with candied fruits or marzipan fruits.

Sprinkle entire top and sides with chopped nuts or Baker's Angel Flake Coconut.

Sprinkle top only with shaved Baker's Unsweetened or German's Sweet Chocolate.

Orange Bread Stuffing

Bread cubes mixed with onions, parsley, seasonings, and concentrated orange juice. A delight with any fowl.

⅔ cup minced onions
½ cup butter
3 tablespoons chopped parsley
¼ cup Birds Eye Concentrated
   Orange Juice
1 teaspoon salt
Dash of pepper
¼ to ½ teaspoon sage
1 teaspoon poultry seasoning
8 cups dry bread cubes

Sauté onions in butter about 3 minutes. Remove from heat and add parsley, concentrated orange juice, and seasonings. Add to bread cubes, tossing lightly with a fork until thoroughly mixed. Makes enough to stuff an 8- to 10-pound fowl.

PREPARE-AHEAD HINT. Make stuffing, cover tightly with foil, and refrigerate. Stuff the fowl just before roasting.

Peach Rice Stuffing

Something different in the way of stuffings. Try also baking in a casserole with chicken breasts on top.

1 package (12 ounces) Birds Eye
   Sliced Peaches, thawed
1⅓ cups fruit juice and water
2 teaspoons salt
Dash of pepper
¾ teaspoon poultry seasoning
1 tablespoon vinegar
1⅓ cups Minute Rice
¼ cup chopped onion
½ cup diced celery
2 tablespoons butter
1 tablespoon chopped parsley

Drain peaches and set aside. Add water

to juice to equal 1⅓ cups and combine with salt, pepper, poultry seasoning, and vinegar in a saucepan. Heat to boiling. Stir in Minute Rice. Cover and remove from heat; let stand 5 minutes.

Meanwhile, sauté onion and celery in butter until onion is transparent. Cut peach slices into thirds. Add sautéed onion and celery, the peaches, and parsley to rice. Mix lightly with a fork. Makes about 1 quart stuffing — enough for a small chicken or duck.

PREPARE-AHEAD HINT. Make stuffing, cover with foil, and refrigerate until ready to use.

Spinach Stuffing

Roll in veal slices or minute steaks, or bake between ham slices, or stuff in tomatoes before broiling.

1 package (10 ounces) Birds Eye
   Chopped Spinach
¼ cup diced celery
2 tablespoons chopped onion
2 tablespoons salad oil
¾ teaspoon salt
⅛ teaspoon pepper

Cook spinach as directed on package. Drain. Sauté celery and onion in salad oil over medium heat until onion is transparent. Add to spinach with salt and pepper. Mix well. Makes ⅔ cup.

PREPARE-AHEAD HINT. Make in advance, if desired, and refrigerate until ready to use.

Onion Rings for Garnish

French fried onion rings, heated until very crisp and used as a garnish.

Spread 1 package (4 ounces) Birds Eye French Fried Onion Rings on baking sheet. Bake in a moderate oven (375°F.) for 10 minutes. Turn onions carefully and bake 5 minutes longer. Cool. Use as a garnish for individual salad bowls or a large tossed salad. Makes enough for 6 individual salad bowls.

Note: Crisp onion rings also make excellent garnish for soft-textured vege-table such as creamed spinach or winter squash. Chopped onion rings serve nicely as garnish for canapés.

PREPARE-AHEAD HINT. Make ahead and serve cold as garnish.

Orange Fluff Sauce (p. 82) complements any fruit or fruit dessert. Try the sauce also with just-thawed berries or peaches.

Lemon Cake Filling

Try with angel food cakes, split into layers, or use to fill cupcakes.

3 tablespoons cornstarch
⅔ cup sugar
Dash of salt
1 cup water
1 tablespoon butter
⅓ cup Birds Eye Concentrated
   Lemonade
Few drops yellow food coloring
1 teaspoon vanilla

Combine cornstarch, sugar, and salt in small saucepan. Add water gradually, stirring constantly. Cook and stir over medium heat until mixture is thickened and clear — about 5 minutes. Remove from heat. Add butter, concentrated lemonade, yellow coloring, and vanilla; blend well. Chill. Makes 1⅓ cups filling, or enough to spread between two 9-inch cake layers.

Lime Cake Filling. Use above recipe but substitute ⅓ cup Birds Eye Concentrated Limeade for the lemonade.

Orange Cake Filling. Use above recipe but substitute ⅓ cup Birds Eye Concentrated Orange Juice for the lemonade.

Orange Cream Cheese Frosting

These are "show-off" frostings — fruit-flavored, colorful and gay, and easy to make.

3 tablespoons butter
1 package (3 ounces) cream cheese
   (at room temperature)
Dash of salt
¼ cup Birds Eye Concentrated
   Orange Juice, thawed
4½ cups sifted confectioners'
   sugar (about)

Cream butter; add cheese, salt, and concentrated orange juice and cream together until light and fluffy. Then gradually add sugar, until frosting is of right consistency to spread, blending well after each addition. Makes about 1⅞ cups frosting, or enough to cover tops and sides of two 8-inch cake layers, or enough for 60 tiny cupcakes — about 1-inch in diameter.

Lemon Cream Cheese Frosting. Use above recipe but substitute ¼ cup Birds Eye Concentrated Lemonade for the orange juice. Add 2 drops yellow food coloring, if desired.

Lime Cream Cheese Frosting. Use above recipe but substitute ¼ cup Birds Eye Concentrated Limeade for the orange juice. Add few drops green food coloring, if desired.

Pink Cream Cheese Frosting. Use above recipe but substitute ¼ cup Birds Eye Concentrated Chill-Ripe Punch for the orange juice.

Tangerine Cream Cheese Frosting. Use above recipe but substitute ¼ cup Birds Eye Concentrated Tangerine Juice for the orange juice.

Grape Cream Cheese Frosting. Use above recipe but substitute ¼ cup Birds Eye Concentrated Concord Grape Juice for the orange juice.

Fruit-Salad Mayonnaise

Fruit concentrates blended into mayonnaise for mixed fruit salads.

2½ to 3 tablespoons Birds Eye
   Concentrated Orange Juice*
1 cup mayonnaise or salad dressing

* Or use Birds Eye Concentrated Lemonade, Limeade, Orange and Grapefruit Juice, Tangerine Juice, Concord Grape Juice, or Grapefruit Juice.

Measure concentrated juice (right from the can) and add to the mayonnaise. Mix well. Serve with fruit salads. Makes about 1 cup, or enough for 6 to 8 servings.

PREPARE-AHEAD HINT. Make ahead and let stand to blend flavors.

Quick Orange Butter

Butter mixed with parsley, chives, and orange concentrate to complement vegetable flavors.

½ cup butter, melted
1 tablespoon minced parsley
1 teaspoon chopped chives
½ teaspoon salt
Dash of cayenne
2 tablespoons Birds Eye Concentrated
   Orange Juice, thawed

Combine ingredients, stirring well. Serve at once over asparagus, broccoli, cauliflower, or spinach. Makes ½ cup.
Fluffy Orange Butter. Use above recipe, but instead of melting the butter, cream it until fluffy and then mix in remaining ingredients.
PREPARE-AHEAD HINT. Fluffy Orange Butter may be made ahead and refrigerated. But the Quick Orange Butter should be prepared just before serving.

Lemon Sauce

A clear lemon sauce with full tangy flavor. Very easy to make with no grating of lemon rind nor juice squeezing.

2 tablespoons cornstarch
¾ cup sugar
Dash of salt
1 cup water
1 tablespoon butter
⅓ cup Birds Eye Concentrated
   Lemonade

Combine cornstarch, sugar, and salt in saucepan. Add water gradually, stirring constantly. Cook and stir over medium heat until mixture is thickened and clear — about 5 minutes. Remove from heat. Add butter and concentrated lemonade; blend well. Serve warm or cold on fruit, cake squares, apple pudding, or gingerbread. Makes 1¼ cups sauce.
PREPARE-AHEAD HINT. Sauce may be cooked in advance and served chilled or reheated just enough to warm. Do not overheat as lemon juice and heat combined sometimes break down the thickening of a cornstarch sauce.

French-Style Fruit Salad Dressing

A dressing with just the right tanginess for fruits.

Measure 1 cup Good Seasons Classic Salad Dressing or other favorite French dressing into a bowl or cruet. Add 1 to 2 tablespoons Birds Eye Concentrated Orange Juice (right from the can). Mix well. Serve with fruit salads. Makes about 1 cup, or 8 to 10 servings. *Note:* If desired, substitute any of these Birds Eye Concentrates for the orange juice: Lemonade, Limeade, Orange and Grapefruit Juice, Grapefruit Juice, Tangerine Juice.

Fruit-Glazed Muffins

With this ingenious quick-trick, muffins glaze as they bake.

Prepared muffin mix
Sugar cubes
Birds Eye Concentrated Orange
   Juice, thawed*

* Or use Birds Eye Concentrated Lemonade, Limeade, Orange and Grapefruit Juice, Grapefruit Juice, Tangerine Juice, or Concentrated Concord Grape Juice.

Prepare muffin mix as directed on package. Spoon batter into well-greased muffin tins. Dip a cube of sugar into concentrated juice and place on top of each muffin, pressing down into the batter. Bake as directed on mix package. Sugar glazes as muffins bake.
For interesting variety, use orange concentrate for a third of the muffins, limeade for another third, and Concord grape juice for the rest.

81

Curried Fruits

A perfect fillip for meats.

1 package (12 ounces) Birds Eye
  Mixed Fruit, thawed
1 package (12 ounces) Birds Eye
  Sliced Peaches, thawed
½ teaspoon curry powder
2 tablespoons brown sugar
1 tablespoon vinegar
4 teaspoons cornstarch
2 teaspoons butter

Combine fruits, curry powder, brown sugar, and vinegar in saucepan. Remove a little of the fruit juice and blend with the cornstarch to form a smooth paste. Stir into fruit mixture. Cook and stir over medium heat until thickened and clear. Stir in butter until melted. Serve hot as an accompaniment to roast pork, beef, or fowl. Makes 3 cups.
PREPARE-AHEAD HINT. Make in advance; reheat at meal-preparation time.

Orange Fluff Sauce

A delicate airy sauce for holidays and other special occasions.

½ cup Birds Eye Concentrated
  Orange Juice
½ cup sugar
Dash of salt
2 egg yolks, slightly beaten
1 cup whipping cream

Combine concentrated orange juice, sugar, and salt in saucepan. Place over low heat and simmer until sugar is dissolved, stirring constantly — about 1 minute. Add a little of mixture to egg yolks, stirring constantly. Then gradually stir egg-yolk mixture into orange-juice mixture in pan. Continue to cook and stir until sauce thickens slightly. Cool. Whip cream and fold into sauce. Serve on steamed chocolate pudding, cottage pudding, angel food cake, or other desserts. Makes 2 cups sauce.

PREPARE-AHEAD HINT. Make sauce with orange juice, sugar, and egg yolks as directed. Just before serving, fold into whipped cream.

Silken Fruit Sauces

These sauces are simply fruits puréed in a blender or forced through a sieve. You'll find dozens of ways to use them.

Use 1 package (10 ounces) Birds Eye Red Raspberries, Birds Eye Sliced Strawberries, or Birds Eye Strawberry Halves or 1 package (12 ounces) Birds Eye Sliced Peaches. Thaw slightly. Then place in an electric blender. Cover. Blend until smooth. Serve over mixed fresh fruits, pudding, ice cream, melon balls, or sherbet.
Note: If desired, thaw fruits completely; force through a sieve or potato ricer.

Poultry Orange Sauce

A spiced orange sauce with currants to serve on goose, duck, or chicken. Delightful on ham, too.

2½ tablespoons sugar
1 tablespoon cornstarch
¼ teaspoon salt
⅛ teaspoon ground cloves
1 cup water
⅓ cup Birds Eye Concentrated
  Orange Juice
2 tablespoons currants
2 tablespoons butter

Combine sugar, cornstarch, salt, and cloves in a saucepan. Gradually stir in water, blending well; then stir in concentrated orange juice. Bring to a boil over medium heat, stirring constantly. Boil 1 minute. Remove from heat; add currants and butter. Serve hot with roast duck or goose. Makes 1 cup.
PREPARE-AHEAD HINT. Make sauce in advance and reheat before serving.

Strawberry Sauce

A thrifty and delicious sauce to serve at community suppers.

3 family size packages (6 ounces each)
  Lemon Jell-O Gelatin
3 cups boiling water
3 cups cold water
3 packages (10 ounces each) Birds Eye
  Sliced Strawberries or Strawberry
  Halves
3 tablespoons lemon juice

Dissolve Jell-O in boiling water. Add cold water, the frozen block of strawberries, and the lemon juice. Stir to separate berries; then chill or let stand at room temperature until mixture is slightly thickened. Serve over ice cream, sponge cake, angel food cake, shortbread biscuits, or puddings. Garnish with a whipped topping, if desired. Makes 40 servings, about ¼ cup each. *Note:* If sauce starts to set up, let stand over hot water and stir until sauce is of right consistency to use.

Yes, it's the same ever-popular chicken, roasted to a turn, but the Peach Rice Stuffing (p. 78) is deliciously different.

It's double fun to make jams for gift-giving when frost and holiday spirit tinge the air. Easy, too, with frozen fruits.

SECTION 8

Jellies and Jams

Probably the first woman to make jellies and jams was mainly concerned with preserving the fruit crop. Today we have quick-freezing — the efficient and modern way to save fruits for winter meals. But still we like a bit of jam for toast or biscuits and a dab of jelly with the roast.

With frozen fruits and concentrates, we can make jams and jellies in convenient amounts — seven or eight glasses at a time — at any season of year. They take up little storage space and there's no frantic rush to preserve the fruits before they spoil.

An easy plan is first to find favorite recipes and then to keep the recipe ingredients on hand, including frozen fruits. Store fruits in the freezer and make up recipes at leisure. For gifts, too. An attractive jar of homemade jelly or jam is an especially friendly gift — and one anybody can afford.

If a batch of jelly or jam lasts less than a month in your family, omit the paraffin and cover the glass top with foil or transparent saran. For longer storage, cover the hot jellies or jams, as soon as poured, with a thin layer of paraffin. Thick paraffin may press down and cause seepage around the edges.

A final tip on paraffin: Always melt it in a pan over hot water. With direct heat the melted wax tends to spatter.

Orange Juice Jelly

Clear, jewel-colored jellies, made with concentrated fruit juices. Yield: about 6 medium glasses.

3¾ cups (1⅔ pounds) sugar
1 box Sure-Jell fruit pectin
2 cups water
1 can (6 ounces) Birds Eye Concentrated
  Orange Juice, thawed — ¾ cup

First, wash, rinse, and scald 6 medium glasses. Set paraffin in saucepan over hot water to melt.

Next, measure sugar and set aside.

Then measure Sure-Jell, water, and concentrated juice into a *large* saucepan and mix well. Cook over high heat until bubbles form all around edge, stirring constantly. Add sugar and cook, stirring constantly, until bubbles again form around edge. Remove from heat. Skim off foam with metal spoon. Pour quickly into glasses. Cover jelly at once with ⅛ inch hot paraffin.

Grape Juice Jelly. Use above recipe, but substitute 1 can (6 ounces) Birds Eye Concentrated Concord Grape Juice for the orange juice.

Chill-Ripe Jelly. Use above recipe, but substitute 1 can (6 ounces) Birds Eye Concentrated Chill-Ripe Punch

and increase water to 2½ cups and sugar to 4 cups (1¾ pounds).

Tangerine Juice Jelly. Use above recipe, but substitute 1 can (6 ounces) Birds Eye Concentrated Tangerine Juice for the orange juice.

Raspberry Jam

A quickly-made jam with the fresh flavor of uncooked fruit. Yield: about 9 medium glasses.

3 packages (10 ounces each) Birds Eye
  Red Raspberries — 3½ cups, thawed
5 cups (2¼ pounds) sugar
1 box Sure-Jell fruit pectin
1 cup water

First, wash, rinse, and scald 9 medium glasses.

Next, crush thawed raspberries and measure into a large pan or bowl. Measure sugar and set aside.

Then mix Sure-Jell and water in a small saucepan. Bring to a *full rolling boil* and *boil hard 1 minute,* stirring constantly. Add to the fruit; then add the sugar and stir for 1 minute. Ladle quickly into glasses or freezer containers. Cover jam at once with tight lids or seals. Let stand 24 hours. Store in freezer, or if jam is to be used within 2 weeks, store in refrigerator.

Raspberry-Pineapple Jam

Wonderful with cream cheese on crackers or as cake filling with a fluffy pale pink frosting. Yield: about 10 medium glasses.

2 packages (10 ounces each) Birds Eye
  Red Raspberries, thawed — 2½ cups
2⅓ cups (1 pound 4 ounces) canned
  crushed pineapple
¼ cup water
5½ cups (2 pounds 6 ounces) sugar
½ bottle Certo fruit pectin

First, wash, rinse, and scald 10 medium glasses. Set paraffin in saucepan over hot water to melt.

Next, prepare fruits: Combine fruits in a *very large* saucepan. Add water and sugar and mix well.

Then make jam: Place saucepan over high heat, bring to a *full rolling boil,* and *boil hard 1 minute,* stirring constantly. Remove from heat and at once stir in Certo. Skim off foam with metal spoon. Then stir and skim by turns for 5 minutes to cool slightly and to prevent floating fruit. Ladle quickly into glasses. Cover jam at once with ⅛ inch hot paraffin. Or if desired, pour jam into freezer containers. Cover at once with tight lids, omitting paraffin. Let stand 24 hours. Then store in freezer. Without paraffin, jam will also keep in refrigerator 2 weeks.

Peach Chutney (p. 89) is a spicy delight to be served with meats and rice dishes. Make extra jars, too, for gift-giving.

Strawberry-Cherry Jam

A deep red jam with slightly tart flavor. Yield: about 7 medium glasses.

2 cups (1 pound 4 ounces) canned
    pitted red sour cherries, water-packed
1 package (10 ounces) Birds Eye
    Sliced Strawberries or Strawberry
    Halves, thawed — 1 cup
3 tablespoons lemon juice — about
    1½ lemons
4½ cups (2 pounds) sugar
½ bottle Certo fruit pectin

First, wash, rinse, and scald 7 medium glasses. Set paraffin in saucepan over hot water to melt.

Next prepare fruit: Drain and chop cherries. Measure and add enough juice

A springtime jam you can make any season with frozen fruits. (See right.)

to make 2 cups. Combine with thawed strawberries in a *large* saucepan. Add lemon juice and sugar and mix well.

Then make jam: Place saucepan over high heat, bring to a *full rolling boil,* and *boil hard 1 minute,* stirring constantly. Remove from heat and at once stir in Certo. Skim off foam with metal spoon. Then stir and skim by turns for 5 minutes to cool slightly and to prevent floating fruit. Ladle quickly into glasses. Cover jam at once with ⅛ inch of hot paraffin.

Strawberry-Rhubarb Jam

A year-round favorite in the jam family. Recipe makes 8 medium glasses.

1 package (1 pound) Birds Eye
    Rhubarb, thawed — 1¾ cups
2 packages (10 ounces each) Birds Eye
    Sliced Strawberries or Strawberry
    Halves thawed — 2¼ cups
½ cup water
4½ cups (2 pounds) sugar
1 box Sure-Jell fruit pectin

First, wash, rinse, and scald 8 medium glasses. Set paraffin in saucepan over hot water to melt.

Next prepare fruit: Chop thawed rhubarb into small pieces. Combine with thawed strawberries and measure 4 cups into a *very large* saucepan. Add the water.

Then make jam: Measure sugar and set aside. Add Sure-Jell to fruit in saucepan and mix well. Place over high heat and bring to a hard boil. At once stir in sugar. Bring to a *full rolling boil* and *boil hard 1 minute,* stirring constantly. Remove from heat and skim off foam with metal spoon. Then stir and skim by turns for 5 minutes to cool slightly and to prevent floating fruit. Ladle quickly into glasses. Cover jam at once with ⅛ inch hot paraffin. *Note:* If you plan to use up jam within a month, omit the paraffin and cover well with foil. Store in refrigerator or other cold place.

For Strawberry-Pineapple Jam, use the following:

1 package (10 ounces) Birds Eye Sliced
    Strawberries or Strawberry Halves,
    thawed — 1 cup
2⅓ cups (1 pound 4 ounces) crushed
    pineapple
¼ cup water
1 box Sure-Jell fruit pectin
3½ cups (1½ pounds) sugar

First, wash, rinse, and scald 8 medium glasses. Set paraffin in saucepan over hot water to melt.

Next prepare fruit: Place berries and juice in a *very large* saucepan. Crush berries slightly. Add the crushed pine-apple and water.

Then make jam as directed for Strawberry-Rhubarb Jam.

Peach Chutney

A well-spiced fruit preserve to serve with meats or rice casseroles. Yield: about 10 medium glasses.

3 packages (12 ounces each) Birds Eye
    Sliced Peaches, thawed
½ cup vinegar
¼ cup lemon juice
1 cup raisins
¼ cup drained slivered preserved ginger
⅓ cup chopped onion
1 teaspoon allspice
½ teaspoon cinnamon
½ teaspoon cloves
½ teaspoon ground ginger
1 tablespoon salt
¾ cup firmly packed dark
    brown sugar
3 cups granulated sugar
1 box Sure-Jell fruit pectin

First, wash, rinse, and scald 10 medium

Jellies made with frozen juice concentrates are jewel clear and true fruit-flavored. Recipe (p. 86) has variations.

glasses. Set paraffin in saucepan over hot water to melt.

Next prepare fruit: Chop thawed peaches into small pieces and place in a *very large* saucepan. Add vinegar, lemon juice, raisins, slivered ginger, onion, allspice, cinnamon, cloves, ground ginger, and salt.

Then make the chutney. Measure brown and granulated sugars and set aside. Add Sure-Jell to fruit in saucepan and mix well. Place over high heat and stir until mixture comes to a hard boil. At once stir in sugars. Bring to a *full rolling boil* and *boil hard 3 minutes,* stirring constantly. Remove from heat and skim off foam with metal spoon. Then stir and skim by turns for 10 minutes to cool slightly and to prevent floating fruit. Ladle quickly into glasses. Cover chutney at once with ⅛ inch hot paraffin.

Just a sample of the many wonderful ways to serve frozen foods outdoors or in. Shown in chafing dish are Pickabacks and on hibachi, Hors d'Oeuvre en Brochette (both on p. 6).

SECTION 9

GENERAL FOODS KITCHENS

Cookout Capers

Nothing tastes quite so specially wonderful as food eaten under the high blue sky, whether served on the beach or in the woods or in your own backyard. Therefore, cookout menus may be quite simple but, of course, never monotonously the same.

Many frozen vegetables cook beautifully over charcoal heat when wrapped in heavy-duty aluminum foil and they serve nicely, right from the foil packet. If you're picnicking away from home, pack your frozen food packets with the perishables that you wish to keep cold. Heavy-duty foil is excellent, too, for lining the fire bowl of your barbecue unit to catch the ashes and grease. Only be careful not to cover air vents.

For backyard cookouts, you can often prepare part of a recipe ahead — a sauce, for instance, to be served over fish or chicken broiled on the outdoor grill.

And one more cookout hint: Provide plenty of *large* napkins. Your family and friends will appreciate your thoughtfulness.

Hot Potato Salad in Foil

Potato patties, heated with diced celery and a French-type dressing in a foil packet over outdoor grill.

1 package (12 ounces) Birds Eye
    Potato Patties
½ cup diced celery
2 teaspoons minced onion
½ teaspoon salt
⅓ cup Good Seasons Classic
    Salad Dressing

Place all ingredients on a double 12x18-inch sheet of heavy aluminum foil. Wrap with a drugstore fold along top and ends. Place the packet on grill over glowing coals.

Cook until potato patties are thawed and all ingredients are thoroughly heated — about 30 minutes. Open foil to test for doneness; if necessary, rewrap tightly and continue cooking. When done, open foil, toss lightly with a fork, and serve. Makes 3 or 4 servings.

Barbecued Chicken

Frying chicken, simmered briefly, marinated several hours in sauce, and then barbecued over an open grill.

1 Birds Eye Frying Chicken,
    partly thawed
¾ cup water
¼ teaspoon salt
Barbecue Sauce*

* Use recipe given at right above or a commercial barbecue sauce.

Separate chicken pieces and place in skillet. Add water and salt. Cover and simmer 15 minutes, turning once. Remove chicken to bowl or glass dish. Cool slightly. Then pour Barbecue Sauce over chicken. Cover and refrigerate. Let stand to marinate a few hours.

To barbecue, arrange chicken, skin side down, on greased grill over glowing coals. Baste with Barbecue Sauce.

Barbecue until tender — about 15 to 25 minutes, turning chicken frequently and basting with the sauce. Serve with remaining sauce. Makes 4 servings.

To make **Barbecue Sauce,** combine 1 cup catsup, ½ cup finely chopped onions, ⅓ cup finely chopped green pepper, ⅓ cup chopped celery, 3 tablespoons cooking oil, 2 tablespoons prepared mustard, 2 tablespoons brown sugar, 1 tablespoon Worcestershire sauce, and 1 teaspoon salt. Cover and simmer 15 minutes, stirring frequently. Makes about 2 cups sauce.

PREPARE-AHEAD HINT. Prepare sauce. Simmer chicken as directed and marinate in sauce until ready to barbecue.

Picnic Chicken

Chicken breasts or thighs, brushed with melted butter, and cooked over an outdoor grill.

2 packages (1 pound each) Birds Eye
    Frying Chicken Breasts,
    partly thawed*
¾ cup water
¼ teaspoon salt
Salt and Pepper
Onion or garlic salt (optional)
Melted butter or margarine
1 tablespoon lemon juice (optional)
1 tablespoon chopped parsley
    (optional)

* Or use 2 packages (1 pound each) Birds Eye Frying Chicken Thighs.

Separate chicken pieces and place in skillet. Add water and salt. Cover and simmer 15 minutes, turning once. Remove from skillet and refrigerate until ready to use.

To grill, season with salt and pepper and onion or garlic salt, if desired. Brush with melted butter or margarine. Place skin side down on greased grill over glowing coals. Cook until tender — about 15 to 25 minutes, turning chicken frequently and basting with melted butter.

Before serving, brush with lemon juice and sprinkle with chopped parsley, if desired. Makes 4 servings.

PREPARE-AHEAD HINT. Simmer chicken as directed. Refrigerate until ready to use. Chop parsley and wrap in foil and squeeze lemon juice, if desired.

Scrambled Eggs with Chicken Livers en Brochette

A pleasant dish for Sunday brunch or family cookout.

1 package (8 ounces) Birds Eye
   Chicken Livers, thawed
3 slices bacon, cut in 1-inch pieces
16 tomato wedges
16 canned mushroom caps
Salt and Pepper
Melted butter
4 eggs, slightly beaten
½ cup milk
½ teaspoon minced onion
½ teaspoon salt
Dash of pepper
¼ teaspoon savory
1 tablespoon butter

Alternate chicken livers, bacon, tomato wedges, and mushroom caps on eight 5-inch skewers. Sprinkle with salt and pepper and brush with melted butter. Cook on grill over glowing coals or in a preheated broiler about 4 inches from the heat, turning once and brushing again with butter. Broil about 8 minutes; (do not overcook).

Meanwhile, combine eggs, milk, onion, ½ teaspoon salt, dash of pepper, and the savory. Heat 1 tablespoon butter in skillet until moderately hot. Add egg mixture. Cook over glowing coals, scraping the cooked portions from the bottom and sides of the pan from time to time with a spatula or spoon. (Do not overcook.)

To serve, place scrambled eggs on heated platter and surround with brochettes. Makes 4 servings.

PREPARE-AHEAD HINT. Skewers may be arranged ahead, covered well with foil, and refrigerated. However, tomatoes lose vitamin C when cut and held.

Barbecued Fish in Foil

Fish cooked with a barbecue sauce in a foil packet over hot coals.

1 package (12 ounces) Birds Eye Cod
   or Hadock Fillets, partly thawed
Melted butter or margarine
Thin onion slices (optional)
Barbecue Sauce

Thaw fish just enough to cut into three pieces. Place each serving on a double piece of aluminum foil and brush with melted butter. Cover with thin slices of onion. Spread generously with Barbecue Sauce. Wrap fish in foil with drugstore fold across top and ends and place on grill over glowing coals. Cook until just tender, turning once or twice. Open foil to test for doneness. Baste fish with more sauce. If necessary, re-wrap and continue cooking. Fish is done when easily flaked with a fork. Serve in the foil with remaining sauce. *To make Barbecue Sauce,* sauté ¼ cup chopped onion in 1 tablespoon butter until onion is transparent. Add ½ cup catsup, 2 tablespoons vinegar, 2 tablespoons water, 1½ teaspoons prepared mustard, ¼ teaspoon salt, and 1 tablespoon brown sugar. Simmer 5 minutes. Makes about 1 cup sauce.

PREPARE-AHEAD HINT. Make sauce and slice onions. Cut fish and wrap in aluminum foil packets with sauce and onions as directed. Keep well refrigerated until ready to use.

Vegetable Fancies

For a gourmet touch to picnic meals, have handy any of these: Garlic salt, celery salt, onion salt; canned broiled mushrooms; canned onions; unsalted peanuts or chopped almonds, toasted in butter. (These can be toasted ahead

93

of time and carried in jar or foil.)

Use any of the salts to season vegetables, French fried potatoes, or potato patties or puffs. Add the mushrooms, nuts, or onions (sliced) to such vegetables as green beans, green peas, Italian green beans, or wax beans just long enough before serving to heat through.

Butter-Boil Vegetables in Foil

Vegetables cooked in an aluminum-foil packet with butter, water, and seasonings. For backyard grill, beach picnics, or other cookout.

Use any of the following Birds Eye vegetables: 1 package (9 or 10 ounces) Whole Kernel Corn, Cut Green Beans, French Style Green Beans, Green Peas, Italian Green Beans, Forkhook Lima Beans or Baby Lima Beans, Mixed Garden Vegetables, Peas and Carrots, Cut Wax Beans.

To cook, place frozen block of vegetables on a double thickness of aluminum foil. Add 2 tablespoons butter or margarine and ½ teaspoon salt. Fold foil across top and one end, using drugstore fold. Through the open end, add 2 tablespoons water — (or ¼ cup for Lima beans). Close tightly. Cook on grill over glowing coals just until vegetable is tender. Open foil to test for doneness and, if necessary, rewrap tightly and continue cooking. Serve from foil packet.

Note: Make separate packet for each package of vegetable.

PREPARE-AHEAD HINT. Remove vegetable from package and place in foil packet with butter and seasonings. Refrigerate until ready to use. Add water just before cooking.

No need to skimp on vegetables for cookouts. Simply prepare your frozen favorites by directions given on this page.

Grilled Vegetables in Foil

Whole kernel corn, green beans, green peas, and wax beans, cooked in aluminum foil without water.

Use any of the following Birds Eye Vegetables: 1 package (9 or 10 ounces) Whole Kernel Corn, Cut Green Beans, French Style Green Beans, Green Peas, or Cut Wax Beans.

To cook, place frozen block of vegetables on double thickness of aluminum foil. Spread with 2 to 3 tablespoons butter or margarine and sprinkle with salt and pepper. Wrap foil, using drugstore fold across top and at both ends. Place on grill over glowing coals. Cook until just tender, 30 to 60 minutes, turning once or twice. Open foil to test for doneness and, if necessary, rewrap tightly and continue cooking. Makes about 3 servings.

Note: Cooking time will vary, depending on type of grill and fuel used.
PREPARE-AHEAD HINT. Remove vegetable from package and place in foil packet with butter and seasonings. Keep refrigerated until ready to use or to take on cookout.

Cookout French Fries

Serve as appetizer with a dip while hamburgers or hot dogs are cooking.

Spread Birds Eye Crinkle Cut French Fried Potatoes or Birds Eye French Fried Potatoes in single layer on aluminum foil. Place on grill over glowing coals. Heat until golden brown and crisp, turning occasionally — takes about 20 minutes. Sprinkle with salt or garlic or onion salt to taste. Serve hot.

Do-It-Yourself Seasoning and Flavoring Guide

If you've ever experimented with flavorings and seasonings, you know that experimenting is part of the fun of cooking. But most beginners — (and even old hands sometimes) — need guiding rules so as not to waste food.

As a starter, get acquainted with various herbs and spices. (Many you can buy in very small jars.) It's the aroma of these seasonings that helps impart a subtle flavor to other foods. You can judge somewhat from the fragrance of the herbs which ones you'll most enjoy in your cooking.

Try your hand first at vegetables, fruits, and fish since these foods are compatible to many flavors.

Use new seasonings sparingly until you gain confidence in your own judgment.

Note that for vegetables and fish — the herbs and spices may be added in several ways: in a white sauce, in melted butter, in lemon juice, in oil and vinegar, as a light sprinkle-on, or as a *bouquet garni* in the cooking water. What is a *bouquet garni?* It is a medley of herbs used for seasoning. Thyme, parsley, and dried bay leaf are always included in a *bouquet garni,* but other herbs may be added as desired. The bouquet must be held together for removing later and is there-fore wound with a string or tied in a cheesecloth bag. It is then cooked with the food to be seasoned and lifted out before the dish is served.

Enhance fruits with spices by adding the spiciness to a topping or sauce. Spices tend to darken some fruit colors. Use almond and mint extracts with fruits for a piquant flavor.

With this guide from General Foods Kitchens, you're on your own. Have fun!

SEASONING SUGGESTIONS FOR FROZEN FOODS

ARTICHOKES

in oil and vinegar with a medley of herbs such as chervil, parsley, tarragon, and thyme

in oil and vinegar and fresh dill

in melted butter or cream sauce with capers or chopped chives

ASPARAGUS

in browned butter with a dash of nutmeg, capers, chopped chives or parsley, or chervil

in cream sauce with a hint of horseradish or grated onion

garnished with a mixture of butter, lemon juice, and snipped parsley

sprinkled with marjoram or thyme

in cream sauce with rosemary, sweet basil, dill, or tarragon

BLACK-EYE PEAS

cooked with a *bouquet garni* of bay leaf, celery flakes, parsley, and thyme and then heated with canned or stewed tomatoes

cooked with a *bouquet garni* of bay leaf, thyme, parsley, whole cloves, and garlic clove

BROCCOLI

in melted butter and garlic salt

in melted butter or cream sauce with capers or curry powder or chopped chives

garnished with a mixture of lemon juice, butter, and tarragon, thyme, or marjoram

97

BRUSSELS SPROUTS

in melted butter and chopped chives

in melted butter, lemon juice, and tarragon, marjoram, or thyme

in cream sauce with a sprinkling of nutmeg or mace

BUTTER BEANS

cooked with a *bouquet garni* of bay leaf, parsley, thyme, and whole cloves and served with melted butter and chopped chive

in melted butter with marjoram, rosemary, sweet basil, or thyme

in cream sauce with hint of curry, basil, or savory

CAULIFLOWER

in melted butter with rosemary, basil, savory, or tarragon or chopped parsley or chives

in cream sauce with hint of chili, ginger, or curry powder or a bit of nutmeg or mace

in cream sauce with sprinkling of chopped parsley or chive

COLLARD GREENS

in oil and vinegar with tarragon

cooked with a *bouquet garni* of bay leaf, celery flakes, parsley, thyme, and whole clove

sprinkled with lemon juice, marjoram, and garlic or onion salt

CORN, WHOLE KERNEL

in melted butter with a dash of chili, curry powder, garlic salt, onion salt, savory, or chopped chives

in cream sauce with a hint of mace, nutmeg, or ground cloves

GREEN BEANS or
ITALIAN GREEN BEANS

cooked with a *bouquet garni* of bay leaf, thyme, and parsley

served with melted butter and a pinch of oregano, rosemary, savory, or chopped fresh dill

in cream sauce, sprinkled lightly with nutmeg or mace

in cream sauce, sprinkled with chopped chives

in oil and vinegar with rosemary, savory, dill, oregano, or marjoram

sprinkled with sesame seeds, toasted in butter

KALE

cooked with a *bouquet garni* of bay leaf, celery flakes, parsley, and thyme and served with butter

served with melted butter, seasoned with onion salt

garnished with a mixture of butter, lemon juice, and tarragon

98

LIMA BEANS

in cream sauce or cream with a pinch of basil, savory, rosemary, chili or curry powder, or mace

in melted butter with onion salt or garlic salt or onion juice

cooked with a *bouquet garni* of thyme, celery flakes, bay leaf, and parsley and served with butter

cooked and then heated with canned tomatoes, seasoned very lightly with oregano

MIXED VEGETABLES

in cream or cream sauce with a nip of savory, chervil, marjoram, or thyme, or onion juice

in cream sauce with a dash of curry or chili powder

in melted butter, seasoned with onion or garlic salt

MUSTARD GREENS

sprinkled with lemon juice and tarragon or grated onion

garnished with a mixture of melted butter, lemon juice, and onion salt

garnished with melted butter and a pinch of savory

OKRA

cooked with a *bouquet garni* of bay leaf, thyme, parsley, cloves, and garlic clove and then heated with canned tomatoes

in melted butter with a dash of nutmeg or mace -

PEAS

in melted butter with chopped mint, chopped chives, marjoram, or savory, or chopped parsley

in cream or cream sauce mixed with savory, chopped chives, a dash of nutmeg, mace, allspice, or curry powder

PEAS AND CARROTS

in melted butter with chopped mint, parsley, or chive

in cream or cream sauce with chervil, chopped parsley, dill, thyme, or a pinch of oregano

POTATOES

sprinkled lightly with thyme, chopped chives, chopped parsley, or snipped fresh dill

seasoned with onion or garlic salt

SPINACH

sprinkled with lemon juice and tarragon or grated onion

in melted butter mixed with rosemary, marjoram, nutmeg, basil, savory, or mace

in cream sauce, seasoned with onion or garlic salt or marjoram, rosemary, and basil

in cream sauce, sprinkled with nutmeg or chopped mint or chives

SQUASH (CROOKNECK)

seasoned with garlic salt

sprinkled with marjoram or basil

cooked and then heated with canned tomatoes and seasoned with a bit of oregano

SQUASH (WINTER)

sprinkled with cinnamon, nutmeg, allspice, or ground cloves

seasoned with onion salt

sprinkled with chopped chives

SUCCOTASH

sprinkled with savory, nutmeg, basil, or chopped chives

seasoned with onion or garlic salt

TURNIP GREENS

sprinkled with lemon juice and dill, basil, tarragon, or fennel

garnished with a mixture of butter, lemon juice, and onion salt

YAMS, CANDIED

sprinkled lightly with nutmeg, cinnamon, ground cloves, or allspice

FISH FILLETS

poached with a *bouquet garni* of bay leaf, basil, parsley, and thyme

brushed with melted butter, sprinkled with basil, thyme, or savory, and then baked

served with melted butter and chervil, chopped chives, or capers

served with a mixture of lemon juice, melted butter, and chopped fresh dill

garnished with a cream sauce, seasoned lightly with savory

spread with tomato paste, lightly seasoned with oregano, and baked

MELON BALLS

sprinkled with chopped mint

MIXED FRUITS

garnished with whipped dessert topping or whipped cream and sprinkled with grated nutmeg or chopped candied ginger

garnished with whipped dessert topping or whipped cream, flavored with almond or mint extract

PEACHES

served with whipped dessert topping or thin custard sauce, spiced with cinnamon

flavored with a few drops of almond or orange extract

RHUBARB

mixed with a dash of clove or cinnamon or nutmeg

STRAWBERRIES

sprinkled with chopped mint

garnished with whipped dessert topping and sprinkled with candied ginger or grated nutmeg

garnished with whipped dessert topping, flavored with almond, mint, or orange extract

Index

Accompaniments
Curried Fruits, 82
For entrées, 10
Ambassador Peach Tarts, 64
Ambassador Raspberry Tarts, 64
Ambassador Strawberry Tarts, 64
Angel Pudding, 65
Antipasto, Artichoke, 4
Antipasto, Italian Green Bean, 3
Appetizers
Artichoke Antipasto, 4
Artichoke Hearts in Marinade, 3
Chicken Liver Paté, 6
Fish Bites Hors d'Ouevres, 4
Garnishes for, 1-2
Hearty Beef-Vegetable Chowder, 2
Hors d'Oeuvre en Brochette, 6-7
Italian Green Bean Antipasto, 3
Party Dip, 5
Pickabacks, 6
Quick Clam Bisque, 3
Six O'Clock Canapés, 4
Spinach Hors d'Oeuvre Spread, 6
Two-Tone Paté, 6
Vegetable Blender Soups, 2
Artichoke Antipasto, 4
Artichoke Casserole Poulet, 19
Artichoke Hearts in Marinade, 3
Artichokes Benedict, 15

Artichokes, recipes using, 3, 4, 15, 19, 40, 48, 50
Asparagus and Almond Sauce, 33
Asparagus, recipes using, 22, 23, 31, 32, 33, 35, 42, 50
Asparagus Soufflé, 22
Asparagus-Stuffed Eggplant, 35
Asparagus-Stuffed Tomatoes, 32

Baked Fish with Tomato Sauce, 27
Barbecued Chicken, 92
Barbecued Fish in Foil, 93
Barbecue Sauce (for chicken), 92
Barbecue Sauce (for fish), 93
Bean-Corn-and-Celery Salad, 49
Beef, recipes using, 2, 11, 12, 13, 14
Beef Stew Supreme, 12
Beverages
See **Fruit Drinks**
Bisque, Quick Clam, 3
Blender Recipes, 2, 3, 5, 70, 74, 82
Blueberry Cottage Pudding, 60
Bouquet Garni, 96, 97, 98, 99, 100
Braised Breast of Lamb, 16
Broccoli Grill, 22
Broccoli Italienne, 32
Broccoli, recipes using, 2, 18, 20, 22, 31, 32, 42

Broccoli-Stuffed Tomatoes, 32
Broiled Fish with Cucumber Sauce, 26
Butter-Boil Directions for Vegetables, 41
Butter-Boil Vegetables in Foil, 94
Butter, Fluffy Orange, 81
Butter, Quick Orange, 81

Cakes, 57, 58, 59
Canapés
See **Appetizers**
Casseroles, 11, 12, 19, 20, 22, 24, 31, 32, 34, 36, 37, 38
Cauliflower, recipes using, 36, 37, 42, 48, 50
Cauliflower and Tomatoes, 37
Charts
Frozen Foods, Best Sources of Nutrients, *inside cover*
Maximum Length of Storage for Frozen Foods, *inside cover*
Thawing Times, *inside cover*
Cheese Crust, 24
Cheese, recipes using, 4, 5, 10, 11, 12, 18, 19, 20, 21, 22, 23, 24, 32, 35, 36, 37, 38, 39, 41, 46, 51, 80
Cheese-Vegetable Sauce, 21
Chef's Summer Salad, 50
Chicken and Vegetables in Cream, 18

Chicken Cosmopolitan, 20
Chicken Liver Paté, 6
Chicken Livers, Curried, 21
Chicken Livers en Brochette, Scrambled Eggs with, 93
Chicken, recipes using, 17, 18, 19, 20, 24, 51, 92
Chicken, South German Style, 19
Chicken-Vegetable Casserole, 18
Chill-Ripe Jelly, 86
Chill-Ripe Punch, recipes using, 60, 65, 70, 71, 72, 74, 80, 86
Chowder, Hearty Beef Vegetable, 2
Chutney, Peach, 89
Clam Bisque, Quick, 3
Classic Bleu Cheese Dressing, 50
Cobbler, Rhubarb, 60
Cobbler, Strawberry-Rhubarb, 60
Coconut Peach Melba, 57
Coeur á la Creme, 66
Cookout French Fries, 95
Cookout Recipes
　Barbecued Chicken, 92
　Barbecued Fish in Foil, 93
　Butter-Boil Vegetables in Foil, 94
　Cookout French Fries, 95
　Grilled Vegetables in Foil, 95
　Hot Potato Salad in Foil, 92
　Picnic Chicken, 92
　Scrambled Eggs with Chicken Livers en Brochette, 93
　Vegetable Fancies, 93, 94
Corn and Green Beans in Cheese Sauce, 39
Corn and Peas in Cream, 39
Corn Pudding, 37
Corn, recipes using, 2, 37, 38, 39, 42, 49, 94, 95
Crab Meat Artichoke Salad, 48

Crab Meat au Gratin, 24
Cream Cheese and Peach Salad, 46
Creamed Dried Beef with Vegetables, 13
Creamed Peas and Mushrooms, 38
Creamy Hashed Browned Potatoes, 40
Creative Touch, The, 30
Creole Lima Beans, 36
Crisscross Pie, 61
Cucumber Sauce, 26
Curried Chicken Livers, 21
Curried Fruits, 82
Curried Vegetable Salad, 52-53
Custard Sauce, 65

Desserts
　Ambassador Peach Tarts, 64
　Ambassador Raspberry Tarts, 64
　Ambassador Strawberry Tarts, 64
　Angel Pudding, 65
　Blueberry Cottage Pudding, 60
　Coconut Peach Melba, 57
　Coeur á la Creme, 66
　Crisscross Pie, 61
　Double Strawberry, 63
　Fruit Medley, 56
　Garnishes for, 56
　Ginger Orange Whip, 65
　Hawaiian Ambrosia, 56
　Jellied Medley, 64
　Lemon Meringue Pie, 63
　Lemon Sponge Pudding, 66
　Miracle Peach Pie, 62
　Miracle Strawberry Pie, 61
　Mixed Fruit Ambrosia, 56
　Pastel Snow, 65
　Peach-and-Lemon, 64
　Peaches-in-Shells, 57
　Peach-Mincemeat Pie, 62
　Peach Upside Down Cake, 57

Pilgrim Cups, 67
Quick Fruited Gelatin, 63
Rainbow Tea Cakes, 59
Raspberry-Apple Pie, 64
Raspberry Bavarian Pie, 62
Raspberry-Glazed Cheesecake, 58
Rhubarb Cobbler, 60
Strawberry-Filled Dessert Pancakes, 67
Strawberry-Rhubarb Cobbler, 60
Strawberry-Rhubarb Pie, 61
Strawberry Shortcake, 58
Summer Refresher, 56
Tropical Ambrosia, 56
Deviled Egg Casserole, 22
Dip, Party, 5
Dip, Piquant, 4
Dixie Peas, 34
Do-It-Yourself Seasoning and Flavoring Guide, 96-101
Double Strawberry, 63
Dried Beef, Creamed 13

Egg Dishes, 21, 22, 23, 93
Eggplant, Asparagus-Stuffed, 35
Entrées
　Accompaniments for, 10
　Artichoke Casserole Poulet, 19
　Artichokes Benedict, 15
　Asparagus Soufflé, 22
　Baked Fish with Tomato Sauce, 27
　Barbecued Chicken, 92
　Barbecued Fish in Foil, 93
　Beef Stew Supreme, 12
　Braised Breast of Lamb, 16
　Broccoli Grill, 22
　Broiled Fish with Cucumber Sauce, 26
　Chicken-Vegetable Casserole, 18
　Chicken and Vegetables in Cream, 18
　Chicken Cosmopolitan, 20

Chicken, South German
Style, 19
Crab Meat au Gratin, 24
Creamed Dried Beef
with Vegetables, 13
Curried Chicken Livers,
21
Deviled Egg Casserole,
22
Fillets with Egg-Mustard
Sauce, 24
Fluffy Chive Omelet, 21
Frankfurter Meal-in-
One, 11
Garnishes for, 9
Glazed Ham, 14
Glazed Pork Roast,
14-15
Grape-Glazed
Frankfurters, 11
Green Bean Rarebit
with Baked Potatoes,
23
Ham and Green Bean
Rolls, 12
Hamburgers Piquant, 13
Lamb and Green Bean
Stew, 16
Liver á la Suisse, 20
Meal-in-One Supper
Dish, 10
Orange-Glazed Broilers
with Onions, 17
Orange-Glazed Ham
Slices with Onions, 17
Orange-Glazed Lamb
Chops with Onions, 17
Orange-Glazed Pork
Chops with Onions,
17
Patio Meat Balls, 14
Picnic Chicken, 92
Scrambled Eggs with
Chicken Livers en
Brochette, 93
Short Ribs Supreme, 11
Shrimp Wiggle, 27
Smothered Chicken, 20
Spinach-Stuffed Ham
Slices, 13
Supper au Gratin, 24
Supper Pie, 23
Sweet-Sour Spareribs
and Beans, 15
Swiss Veal with Limas,
17

Tangerine-Glazed
Frankfurters, 10
Tuna au Gratin, 24
Turkey-Vegetable
Casserole, 18
Veal Roulades, 17

Fillets with Egg-Mustard
Sauce, 24
Fillings
Lemon Cake Filling, 80
Lime Cake Filling, 80
Orange Cake Filling, 80
Fish Bites Hors d'Oeuvre,
4
Fish, recipes using, 4, 6,
24, 26, 27, 48, 49, 93
See also Sea Food
Fluffy Chive Omelet, 21
Fluffy Orange Butter, 81
Frankfurter Meal-in-One,
11
French Fries, Cookout, 95
French-Style Fruit Salad
Dressing, 81
Frostings
Garnishes for, 77
Grape Cream Cheese
Frosting, 80
Lemon Cream Cheese
Frosting, 80
Lime Cream Cheese
Frosting, 80
Orange Cream Cheese
Frosting, 80
Pink Cream Cheese
Frosting, 80
Tangerine Cream
Cheese Frosting, 80
Frozen Foods, Best
Sources of Nutrients,
inside cover
Fruit Drinks
Fruit Zip, 72
Garnishes for, 69-70
Grape Sparkler, 70
Harvest Mist, 70-71
Lemon Soft Drink, 70
Lime Soft Drink, 70
Orange Frosted, 70
Orange Sparkler, 70
Pink Punch, 73
Strawberry Punch, 74
Tea Punch, 74-75
Tropical Mist, 71

Tropical Pink Limeade,
72
Fruit-Glazed Muffins, 81
Fruit Medley, 56
Fruit-Salad Mayonnaise,
80
Fruit Zip, 72

Garnishes
For appetizers, 1-2
For desserts, 56
For entrées, 9
For frostings, 77
For fruit drinks, 69-70
For punch bowls, 70
For salads, 46
For soups, 1-2
Onion Rings for garnish,
78
Potato Topping, 39
Gelatin Recipes, 46, 47,
62, 63, 64, 65, 66, 83
Ginger Orange Whip, 65
Glazed Ham, 14
Glazed Pork Roast, 14-15
Glaze, Raspberry, 58
Grape Cream Cheese
Frosting, 80
Grapefruit Juice, recipes
using, 14, 20, 65, 72,
80, 81
Grape-Glazed
Frankfurters, 11
Grape Juice Jelly, 86
Grape Juice, recipes using,
11, 12, 65, 70, 72, 80,
81, 86
Grape Sparkler, 70
Greek Cauliflower Salad,
48
Green Bean Rarebit with
Baked Potatoes, 23
Green Beans Amandine, 31
Green Beans, recipes using
3, 10, 11, 12, 16, 23,
24, 31, 33, 34, 39, 40
41, 42, 50, 52, 94, 95
Green Peas, recipes using,
13, 14, 18, 24, 27, 33,
34, 38, 39, 41, 42, 49,
51, 52, 94, 95
Grilled Vegetables in Foil,
95

Ham and Green Bean
Rolls, 12

Ham, recipes using, 12, 13, 14, 15, 17, 35, 51
Hamburgers Piquant, 13
Harvest Mist, 70
Hawaiian Ambrosia, 56
Hearty Beef-Vegetable Chowder, 2
Herbs
  See Seasoning Guide, 96-101
High Altitude Cookery
  Butter-Boil Directions for Vegetables, 42-43
  Rule of Thumb for High Altitude Cookery, 43
Hors d'Oeuvres
  See **Appetizers**
Hors d'Oeuvre en Brochette, 6-7
Horse-Radish Limas in Cream, 35
Horse-Radish Cream Sauce, 14
Hot Potato Salad in Foil, 92

Iron, best frozen food sources, *inside cover*
Italian Green Bean Antipasto, 3
Italian Green Beans and Water Chestnuts, 31

Jams and Jellies
  Chill-Ripe Jelly, 86
  Grape Juice Jelly, 86
  Orange Juice Jelly, 86
  Peach Chutney, 89
  Raspberry Jam, 86
  Raspberry-Pineapple Jam, 87
  Strawberry-Cherry Jam, 88
  Strawberry-Pineapple Jam, 89
  Strawberry-Rhubarb Jam, 88
  Tangerine Juice Jelly, 86
Jellied Medley, 64
Jellied Raspberry Special, 46
Jellied Vegetables in Sour Cream, 47

Jellies
  See **Jams and Jellies**

Lamb and Green Bean Stew, 16
Lamb, recipes using, 16, 17
Large Recipes (10 to 30 or more servings)
  Angel Pudding, 65
  Bean-Corn-and-Celery Salad (party size), 49
  Chicken-Vegetable Casserole, 18
  Coeur á la Creme, 66
  Crab Meat au Gratin, 24
  Curried Chicken Livers, 21
  Curried Vegetable Salad, 52-53
  Double Strawberry, 63
  Frankfurter Meal-in-One, 11
  Glazed Ham, 14
  Glazed Pork Roast, 14-15
  Large Vegetable Salad, 50
  Patio Salad, 51
  Peach-and-Lemon, 64
  Pink Punch, 73
  Quick Fruited Gelatin, 63
  Rainbow Tea Cakes, 59
  Raspberry-Glazed Cheesecake, 58
  Shrimp-and-Rice Patio Salad, 49
  Six-O'Clock Canapés, 4
  Squash and Onion Savory, 35
  Strawberry-Grapefruit Chill, 47
  Strawberry Punch, 74
  Strawberry Sauce, 83
  Supper au Gratin, 24
  Tea Punch, 74-75
  Tuna au Gratin, 24
  Turkey-Vegetable Casserole, 18
  Two-Tone Paté, 6
Large Vegetable Salad, 50
Lemon Cake Filling, 80
Lemonade, recipes using, 14, 15, 63, 65, 66, 70, 71, 72, 73, 74, 80, 81
Lemon Cream Cheese Frosting, 80
Lemon Meringue Pie, 63
Lemon Sauce, 81
Lemon Soft Drink, 70
Lemon Sponge Pudding, 66
Lima Beans, recipes using, 5, 13, 17, 24, 35, 36, 38, 41, 42, 49, 53, 94
Lime Cake Filling, 80
Lime Cream Cheese Frosting, 80
Lime Soft Drink, 70
Limeade, recipes using, 14, 65, 66, 70, 72, 74, 80, 81
Liver á la Suisse, 20
Luncheon Salad, 52
Lyonnaise Vegetable Casserole, 36-37

Marinated Vegetables, 40
Maximum Length of Storage for Frozen Foods, *inside cover*
Mayonnaise, Fruit-Salad, 80
Meal-in-One Supper Dish, 10
Meat Balls, Patio, 14
Meat Recipes
  Beef Stew Supreme, 12
  Braised Breast of Lamb, 16
  Creamed Dried Beef with Vegetables, 13
  Glazed Ham, 14
  Glazed Pork Roast, 14-15
  Grape-Glazed Frankfurters, 11
  Ham and Green Bean Rolls, 12
  Hamburgers Piquant, 13
  Lamb and Green Bean Stew, 16
  Liver á la Suisse, 20
  Meal-in-One Supper Dish, 10
  Orange-Glazed Ham Slices with Onions, 17
  Orange-Glazed Lamb Chops with Onions, 17
  Orange-Glazed Pork Chops with Onions, 17
  Patio Meat Balls, 14

Short Ribs Supreme, 11
Spinach-Stuffed Ham
  Slices, 13
Sweet-Sour Spareribs
  and Beans, 15-16
Swiss Veal with Limas,
  17
Tangerine-Glazed
  Frankfurters, 10
Veal Roulades, 17
Miracle Peach Pie, 62
Miracle Strawberry Pie,
  61
Mixed Fruit Ambrosia, 56
Mixed Fruit, recipes using,
  56, 61, 64, 82
Mixed Vegetables, recipes
  using, 2, 13, 21, 36,
  41, 42, 94
Muffins, Fruit-Glazed, 81
Mushroom Sauce, 19

Nutrients, best frozen
  food sources, *inside
  cover*

Okra Pilaf, 40
Omelet, Fluffy Chive, 21
Onion Rings for Garnish,
  78-79
*Orange and Grapefruit
  Juice,* recipes using,
  12, 14, 65, 72, 80, 81
Orange Bread Stuffing, 78
Orange Cake Filling, 80
Orange Cream Cheese
  Frosting, 80
Orange Fluff Sauce, 82
Orange Frosted, 70
Orange-Glazed Broilers
  with Onions, 17
Orange-Glazed Ham
  Slices with Onions, 17
Orange-Glazed Lamb
  Chops with Onions,
  17
Orange-Glazed Pork
  Chops with Onions,
  17
Orange Juice Jelly, 86
Orange Juice, recipes
  using, 4, 14, 17, 65,
  66, 70, 71, 72, 73, 78,
  80, 81, 82, 86
Orange Sparkler, 70

Oriental Patio Salad, 51
Outdoor Recipes
  See **Cookout Recipes**
Oven Directions for
  Vegetables, 42

Pancakes, Potato, 40
Pancakes, Strawberry-
  Filled Dessert, 67
Paraffin Tips, 86
Party Dip, 5
Pastel Snow, 65
Paté, Chicken Liver, 6
Paté, Two-Tone, 6
Patio Meat Balls, 14
Patio Salad, 51
Peach-and-Lemon, 64
Peach Chutney, 89
Peaches, recipes using, 46,
  57, 62, 64, 74, 78, 82,
  89
Peaches-in-Shells, 57
Peach-Mincemeat Pie, 62
Peach Rice Stuffing, 78
Peach Upside Down Cake,
  57
Peas and Carrots, recipes
  using, 16, 38, 41, 42,
  47, 51, 94
Peas Savory, 34
Pickabacks, 6
Picnic Chicken, 92
Pies, One-Crust, 23, 61,
  62, 63
Pies, Two-Crust, 61, 62,
  64
Pilgrim Cups, 67
Pink Cream Cheese
  Frosting, 80
Pink Punch, 73
Piquant Dip, 4
Pork, recipes using, 14, 15,
  17
Potatoes and Cheese, 41
Potatoes, Baked, with
  Green Bean Rarebit,
  23
Potato Pancakes, 40
Potatoes, recipes using, 2,
  3, 6, 11, 23, 39, 40,
  41, 46, 92, 95
Potato Topping, 39
Poultry Orange Sauce, 82
Poultry, recipes using, 17,
  18, 19, 20, 24, 51, 92

Protein, best frozen food
  sources, *inside cover*
Puddings, 60, 65, 66, 67
Punches, 73, 74

Quantity Recipes
  See Large Recipes
Quick Clam Bisque, 3
Quick Fruited Gelatin, 63
Quick Orange Butter, 81

Rainbow Tea Cakes, 59
Rarebit, Green Bean, 23
Raspberries, recipes using,
  46, 57, 58, 62, 63, 64,
  65, 74, 82, 86, 87
Raspberry-Apple Pie, 64
Raspberry Bavarian Pie,
  62
Raspberry Glaze, 58
Raspberry-Glazed
  Cheesecake, 58
Raspberry Jam, 86
Raspberry-Pineapple Jam,
  87
Rhubarb Cobbler, 60
Rhubarb, recipes using,
  60, 61, 88
Rice, recipes using, 24,
  31, 33, 40, 49, 51, 52
Rule of Thumb for High
  Altitude Cookery, 43

Salad Dressings
  Classic Bleu Cheese
    Dressing, 50
  French-Style Fruit Salad
    Dressing, 81
  Fruit-Salad Mayonnaise,
    80
  Vinaigrette Dressing, 50
Salads
  Garnishes for, 46
  Jellied
    Cream Cheese and
      Peach Salad, 46
    Jellied Raspberry
      Special, 46
    Jellied Vegetables in
      Sour Cream, 47
    Strawberry-Grapefruit
      Chill, 47

106

Meat or Poultry
  Chef's Summer Salad, 50
  Oriental Patio Salad, 51
  Patio Salad, 51
Sea Food
  Crab Meat Artichoke Salad, 48
  Shrimp-and-Rice Patio Salad, 49
Vegetable
  Bean-Corn-and-Celery Salad, 49
  Curried Vegetable Salad, 52-53
  Greek Cauliflower Salad, 48
  Hot Potato Salad in Foil, 92
  Large Vegetable Salad, 50
  Luncheon Salad, 52
  Salad Vinaigrette, 50
  Wax Bean Salad, 47
Salad Vinaigrette, 50
Sauces, Cocktail
  Piquant Dip, 4
Sauces, Dessert
  Custard Sauce, 65
  Lemon Sauce, 81
  Orange Fluff Sauce, 82
  Silken Fruit Sauces, 82
  Strawberry Sauce, 83
  Tropical Sauce, 60
Sauces, Entrée
  Barbecue Sauce (for chicken), 92
  Barbecue Sauce (for fish), 93
  Cheese-Vegetable Sauce, 21
  Cucumber Sauce, 26
  Horse-Radish Cream Sauce, 14
  Mushroom Sauce, 19
  Poultry Orange Sauce, 82
Sauces, Vegetable
  Fluffy Orange Butter, 81
  Quick Orange Butter, 81
  Vinaigrette Dressing, 50
Sausage, recipes using, 10, 11

Savory Wax Beans and Rice, 31
Scrambled Eggs with Chicken Livers en Brochette, 93
Sea Food, recipes using, 6, 24, 27, 48, 49
  See also Fish
Seasoning and Flavoring Guide, 96-101
Short Ribs Supreme, 11
Shrimp-and-Rice Patio Salad, 49
Shrimp Wiggle, 27
Silken Fruit Sauces, 82
Six O'Clock Canapés, 4
Smothered Chicken, 20
Sodium-low fruits and vegetables, *inside cover*
Soufflé, Asparagus, 22
Soups, 2, 3
Spareribs, Sweet-Sour, 15
Spices
  See Do-It-Yourself Seasoning and Flavoring Guide
Spinach Casserole, 32
Spinach Hors d'Oeuvre Spread, 6
Spinach, recipes using, 2, 6, 13, 17, 22, 23, 32, 33, 42, 78
Spinach Ring, 33
Spinach-Stuffed Ham Slices, 13
Spinach-Stuffed Tomatoes, 32
Spinach Stuffing, 78
Spring Corn, 37
Squash and Onion Savory, 35
Squash Baked with Marshmallows, 34-35
Squash, recipes using, 34, 35, 42, 67
Stew, Lamb and Green Bean, 16
Stew Supreme, Beef, 12
Storage of Frozen Foods, *inside cover*
Strawberries, recipes using, 47, 58, 60, 61, 63, 64, 65, 66, 67, 74, 82, 83, 88, 89

Strawberry-Cherry Jam, 88
Strawberry-Filled Dessert Pancakes, 67
Strawberry-Grapefruit Chill, 47
Strawberry-Pineapple Jam, 89
Strawberry Punch, 74
Strawberry-Rhubarb Cobbler, 60
Strawberry-Rhubarb Jam, 88
Strawberry-Rhubarb Pie, 61
Strawberry Sauce, 83
Strawberry Shortcake, 58
Stuffings
  Orange Bread Stuffing, 78
  Peach Rice Stuffing, 78
  Spinach Stuffing, 78
Succotash, recipes using, 14, 18, 42
Summer Refresher, 56
Supper au Gratin, 24
Supper Pie, 23
Sweet-Sour Spareribs and Beans, 15
Swiss Veal with Limas, 17

Tangerine Cream Cheese Frosting, 80
Tangerine-Glazed Frankfurters, 10
Tangerine Juice Jelly, 86
Tangerine Juice, recipes using, 10, 14, 65, 70, 72, 80, 81, 86
Tarts, Ambassador Peach, 64
Tarts, Ambassador Raspberry, 64
Tarts, Ambassador Strawberry, 64
Tea Punch, 75
Thawing Times, *inside cover*
Tomatoes, Asparagus-Stuffed, 32
Tomatoes, Broccoli-Stuffed, 32
Tomatoes, Spinach-Stuffed, 32
Tomato Vegetable Casserole, 38

Tropical Ambrosia, 56
Tropical Mist, 71
Tropical Pink Limeade, 72
Tropical Sauce, 60
Tuna au Gratin, 24
Turkey-Vegetable
  Casserole, 18
Two-Tone Paté, 6

Veal, recipes using, 17
Veal Roulades, 17
Vegetable Blender Soups,
  2
Vegetable Casserole
  Royale, 31
Vegetable Fancies, 93-94
Vegetables
  Asparagus and Almond
    Sauce, 33
  Asparagus-Stuffed
    Eggplant, 35
  Asparagus-Stuffed
    Tomatoes, 32
  Broccoli Italienne, 32
  Broccoli-Stuffed
    Tomatoes, 32
  Butter-Boil Directions
    for Vegetables, 41
  Butter-Boil Vegetables
    in Foil, 94
  Cauliflower and
    Tomatoes, 37
  Cookout French Fries,
    95

Corn and Green Beans
  in Cheese Sauce, 39
Corn and Peas in
  Cream, 39
Corn Pudding, 37
Creamed Peas and
  Mushrooms, 38
Creamy Hashed
  Browned Potatoes, 40
Creole Lima Beans, 36
Dixie Peas, 34
Green Beans Amandine,
  31
Grilled Vegetables in
  Foil, 95
High Altitude Cookery,
  42-43
Horse-Radish Limas in
  Cream, 35
Italian Green Beans
  and Water Chestnuts,
  31
Lyonnaise Vegetable
  Casserole, 36-37
Marinated Vegetables,
  40
Okra Pilaf, 40
Oven Directions for
  Vegetables, 42
Peas Savory, 34
Potatoes and Cheese,
  41
Potato Pancakes, 40
Potato Topping, 39
Rule of Thumb for
  High Altitude
  Cookery, 43

Savory Wax Beans and
  Rice, 31
Spinach Casserole, 32
Spinach Ring, 33
Spinach-Stuffed
  Tomatoes, 32
Spring Corn, 37
Squash and Onion
  Savory, 35
Squash Baked with
  Marshmallows, 34
Tomato Vegetable
  Casserole, 38
Vegetable Casserole
  Royale, 31
Vegetable Fancies, 93-94
Vegetables au Gratin,
  38
Vegetable Supreme, 34
Vegetables au Gratin, 38
Vegetables Supreme, 34
*Vegetables, Ways to Vary
  Do-It-Yourself
  Seasoning and
  Flavoring Guide,*
  96-101
The Creative Touch, 30
Vegetable Fancies,
  93-94
Vinaigrette Dressing, 50
Vitamins, best frozen food
  sources, *inside cover*

Wax Bean Salad, 47
Wax Beans, recipes using,
  15, 31, 34, 41, 42, 47,
  94, 95

Maximum Length of Storage
For Frozen Foods

Type of Food	*In Freezer or Freezer Compartment at 0°F.	In Refrigerator Compartment at 10°F. to 20°F.	On Refrigerator Shelf at 45°F.
Cooked Dishes (Pies—Dinners)	1 year	1 month	2 days
Fish and Sea Foods	6 months	1 month	2 days
Fruits	1 year	2 months	3 days
Juice Concentrates	1 year	2 months	6 days
Meats—Pork	6 months	1 month	6 days
Other	1 year	2 months	6 days
Poultry	6 months	1 month	3 days
Vegetables	1 year	1 month	4 days

Note: Foods kept at a constant temperature of 0°F. or less are safe to eat after any length of storage. However, if stored for periods longer than given above at 0°F., there will be loss of freshness, bright color, and peak flavor. Foods kept at 20°F. or less are also safe to eat after any length of storage, but the quality loss is greater. The times given in the chart are meant only as a guide to maximum storage periods. The best — and thriftiest — policy is to keep foods for shorter periods and replace them often.

Frozen foods that have recently thawed should be prepared and served in the same manner as fresh foods.

*As a rule, freezers and refrigerator-type freezers with a separate outside door to freezing compartment maintain a temperature of 0°F. In a compartment without this type door, the temperature is somewhat higher as shown in chart.